Livestreaming

Forerunners: Ideas First

Short books of thought-in-process scholarship, where intense analysis, questioning, and speculation take the lead

FROM THE UNIVERSITY OF MINNESOTA PRESS

EL Putnam
Livestreaming: An Aesthetics and Ethics of Technical Encounter

Dominic Boyer
No More Fossils

Sharad Chari
Gramsci at Sea

Kathryn J. Gindlesparger
Opening Ceremony: Inviting Inclusion into University Governance

J. Logan Smilges
Crip Negativity

Shiloh Krupar
Health Colonialism: Urban Wastelands and Hospital Frontiers

Antero Garcia
All through the Town: The School Bus as Educational Technology

Lydia Pyne
Endlings: Fables for the Anthropocene

Margret Grebowicz
Rescue Me: On Dogs and Their Humans

Sabina Vaught, Bryan McKinley Jones Brayboy, and Jeremiah Chin
The School–Prison Trust

After Oil Collective; Ayesha Vemuri and Darin Barney, Editors
Solarities: Seeking Energy Justice

Arnaud Gerspacher
The Owls Are Not What They Seem: Artist as Ethologist

Tyson E. Lewis and Peter B. Hyland
Studious Drift: Movements and Protocols for a Postdigital Education

Mick Smith and Jason Young
Does the Earth Care? Indifference, Providence, and Provisional Ecology

Caterina Albano
Out of Breath: Vulnerability of Air in Contemporary Art

Gregg Lambert
The World Is Gone: Philosophy in Light of the Pandemic

Grant Farred
Only a Black Athlete Can Save Us Now

Anna Watkins Fisher
Safety Orange

Heather Warren-Crow and Andrea Jonsson
Young-Girls in Echoland: #Theorizing Tiqqun

Joshua Schuster and Derek Woods
Calamity Theory: Three Critiques of Existential Risk

Daniel Bertrand Monk and Andrew Herscher
The Global Shelter Imaginary: IKEA Humanitarianism and Rightless Relief

Catherine Liu
Virtue Hoarders: The Case against the Professional Managerial Class

Christopher Schaberg
Grounded: Perpetual Flight . . . and Then the Pandemic

Marquis Bey
The Problem of the Negro as a Problem for Gender

Cristina Beltrán
Cruelty as Citizenship: How Migrant Suffering Sustains White Democracy

Hil Malatino
Trans Care

Sarah Juliet Lauro
Kill the Overseer! The Gamification of Slave Resistance

Alexis L. Boylan, Anna Mae Duane, Michael Gill, and Barbara Gurr
Furious Feminisms: Alternate Routes on *Mad Max: Fury Road*

Ian G. R. Shaw and Marv Waterstone
Wageless Life: A Manifesto for a Future beyond Capitalism

(Continued on page 86)

Livestreaming
An Aesthetics and Ethics
of Technical Encounter

EL Putnam

University of Minnesota Press

MINNEAPOLIS
LONDON

ISBN 978-1-5179-1709-8 (PB)
ISBN 978-1-4529-7089-9 (Ebook)
ISBN 978-1-4529-7162-9 (Manifold)

Published by the University of Minnesota Press, 2024
111 Third Avenue South, Suite 290
Minneapolis, MN 55401-2520
www.upress.umn.edu

Available as a Manifold edition at manifold.umn.edu

The University of Minnesota is an equal-opportunity educator and employer.

Contents

Context Collapse 1

Zoom Aesthetics 13

Glitch, Noise, and Techno-Grrrls 23

Aesthetics of Duration and
Transformative Justice 37

When Death Goes Viral 49

Patternmaking: Techno-Aesthetics
of Mundane Intimacy 61

Conclusion: (Not) Becoming Machine 73

Acknowledgments 77

Bibliography 79

Context Collapse

Packet-Switching Grief

I said goodbye to my father over a WhatsApp video call in October 2019. He was connected to a ventilator and they were about to pronounce him deceased in an east coast U.S. hospital, as I sat in my home in Ireland over 3,000 miles away. It all happened so suddenly; I was unable to get a flight in time to be there in person for this moment. We had chatted regularly over WhatsApp before that day. Weekly, we would communicate through glitched video and broken sound, sharing the ins and outs of our daily lives. These once magical tools of communication, now commonplace, have enabled us to develop a closeness despite our geographic distance. I never thought I would have to share such an intimate moment—a final goodbye—over livestreamed video.

There was something that felt not quite right about this experience, something inappropriate but also affectively provocative in the desire to connect. Many networked communications technologies are based on packet switching, which is a process of transmission where data is broken down into chunks or packets for more efficient transfer. Originally, it was developed as part of ARPANET, the precursor for the Internet, during the Cold War to decentralize transmissions of data (Baran 1964; Abbate 1999). In this instance, in addition to being the literal means of our connection, it also became a metaphor for my experience of grief, a grief so large it must be broken down into smaller packets to be processed. My poor Internet connection meant that the video was blocky and glitched. I could see my father lying in the hospital bed, though the image translated into chunks of pixels that froze intermittently. At that moment, I felt even further away from him and my family, as the ability to stream over video through this obscured image highlighted our geographic separation (Hunter 2019). It was a sensory encounter of moving image that was also a technologically mediated significant life (and death) event. Finally, I switched to calling over our household landline so my voice was only broken up by cries rather than digital interference.

Not long after this experience, the world entered a period of collective change and grief with the onset of the Covid-19 pandemic in 2020. Around the globe, people experienced parallel moments of drastic loss as systems altered in response to this novel form of the coronavirus. This pandemic has instigated a paradigm shift in public health policy, national governance, engagement with digital technologies, sensors and data collection, social and community development, and individual being. Starting in March 2020, restrictions were placed on geographic movement as it became common for governments around the globe to implement stay-in-place orders, since limiting person-to-person contact was found to be effective in stalling the spread of the virus. A general trend throughout this time was that group events that previously would take place in-person transitioned to livestreamed video. This included types of engagement from various social realms of activity, such as classes, lectures, and other forms of presentation; music, dance, theatre, and other performing arts; job interviews and work meetings; drinking sessions, quiz nights, and family gatherings; and the streaming of funerals and other collective rituals. Suddenly my personal experience of packet-switching grief became common place.

The Great Pivot

In short, when the Covid-19 pandemic began in 2020, digital technologies provided the solution to our synchronous contact needs.

For years now, video livestreaming has enabled visual and aural communication while maintaining physical distancing. Though it did not become widespread until the 2010s, when increased access to web cameras, improved computer hardware, and higher Internet bandwidth enabled the necessary data sharing capacities for this type of communication, the desire to connect through real-time moving image existed in the shared imagination. The 1989 film *Back to the Future II*, set in the year 2015, shows video calls as a regular part of life. Unlike Hover Boards that never materialized as envisioned, technological developments during the twenty-first century, including the advent of the smartphone in 2007 and the capacity to connect to the Internet over cellular networks, have made the ability to communicate live through video omnipresent.

As a performance artist working with digital technologies, when the Covid-19 pandemic began I was intrigued by the capacities of livestreaming and how I could approach this mode of communication as an artistic medium. Livestreaming is appealing because of its real-time contact, the ability to connect with other human beings synchronously while in different locations. Even though video and performance are integral parts of my practice as an artist, I had yet to experiment with live broadcasting. During the first weeks of the pandemic, I watched other artists engage with streaming over social media through performances, informal studio visits to watch someone work on a painting or sculpture, or broadcasting conversations about what it means to produce art in the time of Covid-19, which Irish gallery director and filmmaker Matthew Nevin did in a series called "Matt's Chats" in response to the artistic and social isolation of that time (Nevin 2020). When I staged my first livestreamed performance in April 2020, I was excited about the possibilities. At this point, we had already been in lockdown for about a month. I was coping with our confined context through video—documenting features of my home environment that I otherwise would overlook on a daily basis: the way shadows changed throughout the day, time lapse footage of the garden, and anything that piqued my interest and seemed worth capturing. As I became more familiar with the details of my immediate environment, I longed for the social connections the Internet brings. Livestreaming provided an option to present live performance work, forging a connection with those beyond the home while engaging in artistic activity.

In anticipation of the broadcast, I posted a notification on my various social media accounts, making friends and followers aware of the upcoming performance. I wanted to include some of the videos I had been producing, so for the action, I decided to interact with a video projected onto tracing paper, creating a sort of shadow play that was reminiscent of what I had been documenting around my home. I began the performance, feeling the thrill of the live moment—a sensation I had not experienced in quite some time. There is a rush of adrenaline that accompanies this type of artistic production, where the uncertainty of outcome is intertwined through action, material, context, and witness. As I performed for the camera, breaking up the projected image with the shadows of flowers, I watched familiar names join my stream. Unlike the live performance scenarios in the gallery, where audience members attune to the presented actions for a period of time, I noticed that many of these people who had joined—friends and people I have performed for numerous times—soon left. Watching the playback from the performance, I saw that early on the stream froze, stuck on a single frame for several minutes. Even prior to that technical malfunction, I observed that my actions, which I valued for their subtlety, did not translate well onto the broadcast medium. Time and space are experienced differently through the framing of the camera and the screen—the performed actions that may have proved successful within a gallery context failed when presented as a livestream. Shooting the projected video, which created refracted bands of red, blue, and green when I observed it through my smartphone's screen, compressed poorly through Instagram's platform, appearing as muddy bands. I was disappointed, but also embarrassed at the poor quality of the attempt.

What was striking about the Covid-19 pandemic was not so much the general shift to streaming technologies as a means of synchronous engagement, but the desire to mimic and replicate in-person interactions through technological channels. A term that was used a great deal at the onset of the pandemic was pivot, indicating a rapid change in direction while in motion. To pivot means to rotate or to turn, implying a shift in momentum, but not to stop. That is, digital technologies like livestreaming were engaged with in ways to retain motion during this period of great change. Such types of relations are invariably different, as livestreaming involves mediation by technical objects that create new milieux. Despite these differences, which can be felt through the phenomenological experiences of streaming, there is an ongoing sense of denial that is affiliated with livestreaming—as if the screen can simply take the place of other forms of person-to-person engagement. Stating these differences is not meant to treat livestreaming as an inferior means of communication. Instead, acknowledging how livestreaming is different brings attention to how we engage with these technologies, drawing out possibilities for new modes of connection and access, while also highlighting the forms of restriction and control that are mechanically feasible. It is these factors of difference that serve as the impetus for the current book: how can a study of livestreaming as an aesthetic and ethical encounter enable us to acknowledge the differences that livestreaming introduces to social engagement? How does this impact our relations through and with technical objects? How can we draw from these experiences in order to cultivate novel ecosystems with technologies?

Central to this approach is the understanding that livestreaming functions as a distinctive means of communication and artistic production informed through its technological parameters. Here livestreaming is treated phenomenologically, which is the approach Philip Auslander (2008b; 2012) uses in his extensive research pertaining to liveness and technology. Even though there are qualities of livestreaming that evoke in-person communication, other factors are different. Notwithstanding the ability to see a person's face and communicate in real time, the capacity to read body language is restricted to what can be captured with the camera and presented through the screen. Attention is more focused, as the face is framed and isolated. In a most unusual twist, there is a capacity to view the self when communicating, drawing a heightened awareness to the presentation of self.

Such encounters are social, but also aesthetic and, as I will later discuss, ethical. Aesthetics, however, is not restricted to the production of art nor the stance of the artist. Instead, considering livestreaming as an aesthetic encounter is a means of drawing awareness to the perception of senses and a sharing of the sensible that is experienced through a sensitivity that highlights and forges relations between people, technology, and places. In addition, performance, like aesthetics, is not restricted to artistic contexts, but as Erving Goffman (1959) argued, constitutes our everyday actions and social interactions. Engaging with the philosophy of Gilbert Simondon, I argue that livestreamed internet broadcasts are performed aesthetic and ethical encounters that invite distinctive means of relating to others. Moreover, like the way a performance artist will take non-art materials and situations, transforming them through artistic gestures to become art works, so this book engages with livestreaming in art and non-art scenarios in a similar way through the lenses of aesthetics, ethics, performance theory, media studies, and philosophy.

Simondon, Technology, and Aesthetics

Noted for his influence on Gilles Deleuze, Felix Guattari, Bernard Stiegler, Brian Massumi, Bruno Latour, Elizabeth Grosz, Yuk Hui, and others, Gilbert Simondon is most recognized for his philosophy of technology. His supplementary doctoral thesis *Du mode d'existence des objets techniques (On the Mode of Existence of Technical Objects)*, which was published soon after its completion in 1958, is considered his most influential work. In the past two decades, his theories regarding individuation and ontogenesis as a distinctive approach to ontology and epistemology, as articulated in his main doctoral thesis *L'Individuation à la lumière des notions de forme et de l'information (Individuation in Light of the Notions of Form and Information)*, have gained increased recognition in Francophone scholarship and beyond, as new translations of his texts from French into English expose this thinker's work to a growing audience. Increased interest in Simondon's philosophy beyond France have included anthologies explicating his particular conceptions of being and becoming, such as *Gilbert Simondon: Being and Technology*, edited by Arne De Boever, Alex Murray, Jon Roffe, and Ashley Woodward (2012), as well as the translation of Muriel Combe's insightful introduction to his work, *Gilbert Simondon and the Philosophy of the Transindividual* (2013), and the collection of his lectures edited post-mortem by Nathalie Simondon, *Imagination et Invention* (2014), that has also been recently translated into English (Simondon 2022).

Simondon's philosophy is notable because of his emphasis on becoming, where individuals are not preformed, but experience ongoing phases of development through individuation. In his PhD thesis dedicated to Maurice Merleau Ponty, he critiques hylomorphism, which Aristotle describes as an individual emerging, with an idealized form (*morphe*) in union with matter (*hyle*). Instead, Simondon proposes the concept of ontogenesis, a term appropriated from biology, as an ontological alternative. Here, Simondon argues that individuals are not complete beings, but through processes of individuation (or becoming), an individual is formed through the unfolding of reality. As he states: "we would try to grasp ontogenesis in the whole unfolding of its reality and *to know the individual through individuation rather than individuation starting from the individual*" (emphasis in original, Simondon 2020, 3). Elizabeth Grosz elucidates: "being is at once pre-individual, individuating, and individuated; it becomes something, something emerges or erupts, but it leaves in its context or milieu a residue or excess that is the condition for future becomings" (Grosz 2012, 38). The pre-individual is not a fixed entity that predetermines how an individual comes into being, but is dynamic and supersaturated with potential, as processes of individuation influence through the forces and relations that it gives rise to and acts upon. Relations are not limited to human beings or subjects and objects. Instead, relations include living and nonliving beings through a shared constitutive and constituted milieu, including technical objects. The milieu, which means "middle" in French, is the term Simondon uses in his native tongue to describe the situated existence of technology, where "Man [*sic*] finds himself linked to a universe experienced as a milieu" (Simondon 2016, 177). The continued use of the term milieu in English, rather than translating it to "environment," is significant, as it includes the material environment and the pre-environment, as well as the immaterial relations of "au milieu," or of being "in the middle."[1] Such nuances get lost in translation.

Writing and researching concurrently with cybernetics and systems theory in the mid-twentieth century, Simondon was influenced by this burgeoning field of study. At the same time, Simondon critiques cybernetics, and as Massumi (2012) observes, Simondon's work cannot be considered normative and technocratic. For instance, unlike Claude Shannon (1948) and Warren Weaver (1949), Simondon does not treat information and modes of transmission as dichotomous. He challenges a binary approach that distinguishes form (information) and matter (physical modes of transmission). Rather, he argues that both the content and means of transmission contribute to the transfer of information. Simondon (2016) describes how the technical object should not simply be treated as an instrument or tool–a means to an end–but instead constitutes a technical reality that is integral to human reality and culture, functioning as mediators between the world within which we exist and what we create. His attention to the material properties of technology also distinguishes him from other philosophers of technology, including Martin Heidegger. For instance, at the Lycée Descartes, where he taught in Tours, France from 1948 to 1955, Simondon brought technical objects to the classroom when substi-

---

1. I am grateful for Noel Fitzpatrick for bringing this to my attention.

tute teaching physics classes, extending learning from theoretical insights to include material engagement (Chabot 2014). As Massumi notes, for Simondon, technological innovation is "a key theatre of thought materializing in matter becoming" (Massumi 2012, 20). Throughout his work, Simondon emphasizes the significance of the philosophy of technical objects, an "awareness of the nature of machines, of their mutual relations and of their relations with man [*sic*], and of the values implied in these relations" (Simondon 2016, 19). He calls for a study of technology through the technologist or the mechanologist, as sociology formalizes the study of human relations and psychology formalizes the study of the mind, which treats technical objects as mediators and shapers of human relations that go through their own processes of genesis and concretization. For Simondon, technical objects are involved in the constitution of cultures and situated within their cultural locality. Like aesthetic objects, they tend to be reduced to their utility functions. Humans engage with technical objects through rapport, or relations, with each informing the other through co-constitution. Simondon describes how technology, and specifically technicity as the cultural capacities of tools, "must never be considered an isolated reality, but as part of a system" (Simondon 2016, 170). This system entails relations of objects and nonobjects, living and nonliving beings, constituting its milieu as a realm of experience that leads to states of metastability through phases of being.

Simondon's acknowledgment of technicity in the shaping of human relations is a key factor in why Simondon is the primary interlocutor for this book. He offers a unique approach to aesthetics consistent with his "technical mentality." Simondon provides an in-depth discussion of aesthetics in the third section of *On the Mode of Existence of Technical Objects*, titled the "Essence of Technicity." Throughout this section, Simondon crafts a model of modes of thought, which is divided into phases. In this model, a phase is "not a temporal moment replaced by another," but similar to the phase ratio in physics, results from the splitting of two that exist in a system in relation to each other (Simondon 2016, 173). He differentiates this model from a dialectical model, as there is no need for either succession or negation to fuel conceptions of progress. These phases, therefore, cannot exist in isolation, and therefore no phases contain complete truth or reality. Instead, phases are abstract and partial, existing as a relational system. Simondon describes how technicity arises from the phase shift of a "magical mode," the "unique, central, and original mode of being in the world" (Simondon 2016, 174). Aesthetics is the neutral point that sits at the splitting of magical unity into technics and religion, where "it is not a phase, but rather a permanent reminder of the rupture of unity of the magical mode of being, as well as a reminder of the search for future unity" (Simondon 2016, 174). Aesthetics exists at the cleave between the practical and the theoretical, the scientific and the ethical, imperfectly recalling this lost, magical unity. For Simondon, aesthetics is the way phenomena are experienced through sensation, as processes of becoming and relation.

Aesthetic and Ethical Encounter

In this relational model, Simondon does not treat technical and aesthetic objects as mutually exclusive. Instead, technical objects have the capacity to evoke aesthetic encounters and aesthetics, according to Yves Michaud, "return[ing] us to the heart of technicity" (Michaud 2012, 122). Simondon defines the aesthetic object as:

> the extension of the natural or human world that remains integrated within the reality that bears it; it is an outstanding point in a universe; this point is the result of an elaboration and benefits from technicity; but it is not arbitrarily placed in the world; it represents the world and focalizes its ground forces and qualities, like a religious mediator; it keeps itself in an intermediary state between pure objectivity and subjectivity (Simondon 2016, 199).

The aesthetic object does not need to be an art object or art work in the traditional sense, such as a sculpture or painting; any thing and any experience has the capacity to evoke an aesthetic encounter. Emphasis is placed on the encounter involving the object, the surrounding world, and human gesture, as opposed to just the object itself or the subject's response to it. As an encounter, aesthetics is inherently relational. Technical objects have the capacity to function as aesthetic objects, where its aesthetic qualities manifest when "it extends the world and becomes integrated into it" (Simondon 2016, 197). It is not simply the technical object that instigates this aesthetic experience, but instead it is the technical object in operation that provokes the aesthetic encounter. Such an approach does not reduce aesthetics to form, as Immanuel Kant (2000) proposes in his definition of aesthetic judgement where the subject is disinterested and the object is autonomous. Instead, aesthetics for Simondon emphasizes the *experience* that is affiliated with the aesthetic object, acknowledging its physicality and how it is engaged.

In conjunction with the growing attention to his philosophy more generally, Simondon's approach to aesthetics is also receiving increased interest, though not to the same degree of consideration as his philosophies of technology and individuation. Even Simondon has underestimated the significance of aesthetics, arguing that aesthetics is inferior to philosophy, as aesthetics "refracts aspects of reality, but it does not reflect them" (Simondon 2016, 243). However, Yuk Hui contests Simondon's diminishment of aesthetics as being limited in "expression and communication" when compared to philosophy, arguing that instead "the challenge is not to abandon aesthetic thinking for philosophical thinking, but rather to renew a relation between them" (Hui 2021, 189). Such an approach for Hui does *not* involve developing "a particular techno-aesthetics of virtual reality or machine learning as a solution to the actual problem of technological development" (Hui 2021, 189), which is why this book is not simply a techno-aesthetics of livestreaming. Instead, I am proposing how livestreaming is a performed encounter, with performance understood in the broad sense of the term as a means of doing and interacting, extending beyond the context of artistic production, building upon Simondon's thinking, as I cultivate relations of aesthetics and philosophy that include implications for ethics and politics.

For Simondon, individual beings, both living and physical or nonliving, are relational and incomplete. Throughout his oeuvre, he emphasizes how beings experience processes of differentiation, challenging presumptions regarding form and matter, the psychological and the social, nature and technology. Such relations are wrought with tensions as the "state of the living being is like a problem to be solved, to which the individual becomes the solution through successive assemblages of structures and functions" (Simondon 2020, 226). Simondon describes how individuals and collectives emerge in response to disparation, or the incompatabilities that drive individuation through the need to act to resolve tensions as processes of becoming. In this book, ethics, therefore, are not assessed in terms of virtue, but as a relational ethics of care drawing from feminist and race theory, including the work of María Puig de la Bellacasa (2017), Ruha Benjamin (2022), and Kathleen Lynch (2022). María Puig de la Bellacasa emphasizes how ethics of care "cannot be about a realm of normative moral obligations but rather about thick, impure, involvement in a world where the question of how to care needs to be posed" (Puig de la Bellacasa 2017, 6). As such, ethics are not fixed, but involve hands-on and ongoing processes that entail speculative thinking about what is possible. Moreover, livestreaming functions as an ethical encounter, as well as aesthetic, through techno-social relations that constitute new patterns of being-together as becoming that are complex, ambivalent, and situated, yet also vital for transformation. Treated in such a way, livestreaming exceeds quantifying and calculating metrics, challenges emphasis on content generation, invites paying attention to what typically is not noticed, values the unique phenomenologies of liveness that the medium produces, and introduces new means of social engagement that counter the potentially destructive capacities of automation.

Zoom Aesthetics

OVER THE PAST DECADE, Internet broadcasting and livestreaming have increasingly become a subject of academic study. Much of the existing literature has focused on affective and immaterial labor, especially in relation to the streaming of video games (Woodcock and Johnson 2019), the performance of gender and the specific discriminations faced by femme and women streamers (Guarriello 2019; Zhang and Hjorth 2019), the role of livestreaming in activism (Martini 2018), and the sociological and economic impacts of streaming (Taylor 2018). These studies and analyses focus on live video broadcasting over the Internet with little attention to how aesthetic qualities of livestreaming function in visual culture. Instead emphasis is placed primarily on content, as opposed to how the material and formal parameters of technology frame perception and inform the delivery of content from the approach of art and aesthetics.

In addition, performance studies has tended to shy away from technology, exhibiting what Philip Auslander describes as a "bias toward live events and a resistance to including technologically mediated ones among its objects of inquiry" (Auslander 2008a, 107). Despite the extensive role that technology has long played in the creation and presentation of performance and theatre (Salter 2010), there is a tendency to isolate performance from technology. As with much recent literature from the growing body on the topic of digital technologies and performance, including works by Steven Dixon (2015), Néill O'Dwyer (2021), Nadja Masura (2020), Lindsay Hunter (2021), and my own publication on the topic (Putnam 2022), this current book *centralizes* the role of digital technologies in performance.

According to Simondon's thinking, the relations that livestreaming technologies enable are entangled with technical objects. There are distinctive features to streaming that are unique to this means of communication and how it mediates relations. The typical set-up of the video call is one where a person is sitting in front of the camera. Laptop computers, smartphones, and tablets usually come equipped with a web camera and microphone, which determine how a person will be composed within the image frame. While there are options to alter this set up through the connection of external cameras, including the ability to turn a smartphone into a virtual camera that can be used over streaming platforms like Zoom, the increased ubiquity of cameras and microphones built into devices are standardizing how people generally engage. Typically on a video call, the camera is framed around a person's face, with this person sitting far enough away so that their head and shoulders are visible. Ideally the camera will be placed at eye level, so that conversations are as close to eye-to-eye contact as possible. However, this conversational norm is always skewed through the camera and the screen. If a person were to appear to make eye contact with the person on screen, they would need to be looking into the camera, which means actually avoiding making eye contact with the person on screen in order to appear to be doing so. If the person makes eye contact with the person on the screen, their eyes are shifted in a different direction as they appear to be looking elsewhere and not at the face of the person. In addition, video conferencing and calling software, such as Skype and Zoom, introduce an atypical phenomenon for face-to-face conversations: the ability to look at oneself when conversing. Daniel Miller and Jolynna Sinanan comment upon this aspect of communicating with the webcam as "the very first time that human beings have been able to see who they are" (Miller and

Sinanan 2014, 24). Self-monitoring activates a new perspective of the self, and as such, conversational behaviors adapt to this new mode of engagement that may be unfamiliar in such contexts. No wonder Zoom calls can be so exhausting.

Not only does the webcam and screen draw attention to how one is perceived over the camera, but the space of presentation is also taken into account as livestreaming shifts contexts for conversations. What may have previously taken place in a designated space of work, learning, or leisure is now feasible wherever there is access to the Internet. During Covid-19 lockdowns, this commonly meant conversations would take place within the home environment. Attention to what is on and off camera, both visually and aurally, became widely shared concerns in 2020, as features were introduced to video conferencing platforms to technologically alleviate such issues. For instance, the ability to blur backgrounds or use virtual images means that it is not always necessary to curate a space for livestreaming. Portable light panels and ring lights are used to improve issues with illumination. We are becoming more adept at developing our home broadcast studios, which T. L. Taylor (2018) has observed as a characteristic of gamers who stream over Twitch. Simondon describes how the technical object is the meeting point of two milieux, the technological and the geographic. The engagement of technical objects becomes a negotiation of milieux: "these two milieux are two worlds that do not belong to the same system and are not necessarily completely compatible" (Simondon 2016, 55). It can be argued that the technical objects of livestreaming bring together multiple geographic milieux that are mediated through technologies. With the context collapse of Covid-19, the geographic boundaries that would have facilitated boundaries between different types of work are now merged in a single spatial sphere, an amorphous bubble of labor, connected through the tethers of video streams. These modes of engagement also introduce new forms of intimacy; technology enables communication with others at times and spaces it otherwise may not have occurred. Cameras and microphones allow us to peer into the backstage of our lives. In addition, these devices enter our physical personal space, making visual framing of our persons closer than what we may experience in nonvirtual engagements.

New Forms of Closeness

Such qualities are evident in a livestreamed performance by musician and composer Forbes Graham that occurred in December 2021 as part of the Mobius Artists Group Spiderweb series.[1] While Graham regularly plays the trumpet with digital technologies, extending the range of the instrument and inviting new ways to play it, such an event typically takes place on a stage in a theatre, club, or gallery context, where he plays at a designated distance from a seated audience—a clear division of space between audience and performer measured in physical distribution. For this streamed performance, the screen provides such a division while inviting novel forms of engagement through technology. The audience perspective is framed by the webcam in his laptop, which places the camera slightly below eye level, looking up and within arm's reach. A common distance for verbal communication over livestreaming, the shift of spatial range becomes apparent as he begins to play his trumpet over the camera. The size of the instrument fills the space between his face and the laptop, with the end of the instrument dipping out of the frame of the screen. All we can access are the visual and aural perspective mediated through technology. He manipulates some other technical objects off camera, though it is not possible to observe what he is doing, unlike a stage performance where all his gestures would be visible. We are able to watch his face and fingers as he plays at a distance that is closer than what is possible without a camera present, even closer than the end of the instrument. After his performance, some of the audience members

1. This performance took place as part of the Mobius Spiderweb series. A recording can be viewed on the Mobius website at https://www .mobius.org/video-archive.

comment on the unusual perspective and the closeness that the technology enables—an intimacy drastically different from a theatre or club scenario. The framing is close, and to use Michelle White's (2003) phrasing, too close, bringing attention to details usually observed at a distance, while leaving other actions typically visible off camera. These new forms of intimacy are the negotiation of the shared technical and geographic milieu of this aesthetic encounter.

"Sing the Love of Danger": The Zoom Bomb

Increased engagement with Zoom during the Covid-19 pandemic also brought the Zoom Bomb. During early 2022, I was attending a large, private meeting on Zoom. It was a wellness group that prior to the pandemic would typically meet in-person. At this stage, two years after the start of the pandemic, attending a meeting such as this through livestreaming became a matter of course. What made this one notable though was about fifteen minutes into the speaker's presentation, loud music began to play. Due to the nature of Zoom's set up, it is not possible to speak concurrently, as once a person starts speaking or making noise, that microphone dominates the soundscape. The main person speaking at the meeting continued, his phrases cut through with musical cacophonic intervention. We had been Zoom bombed. Used to such interruptions at this stage, the person in the meeting designated for scanning the room blocked the bomber. Shortly thereafter, noise returned, this time accompanied by an explicit pornographic video displaying bestiality. Faces on the screen conveyed shock. The intruder was again ejected from the room, which soon was followed by another intervention. This time there were no visuals, just the sounds of a person belching. A few more attempts were made to interrupt the meeting with noise and loud music, each time blocked until whomever was disrupting gave up their efforts and moved on. While at this stage I had witnessed a few Zoom bombings, usually presented as explicit text in the chat window or sometimes audible interruptions, this was the first time where

I saw the utilization of intentionally shocking visual material—a video clip that was meant to cause the most damage possible through its graphic shattering of taboos. The persistence of the attempt also stood out, with the bomber (or bombers?) re-entering the room multiple times, attempting over and over again to disrupt our gathering. The bomber(s) engaged with the technical capacities of Zoom that are meant to facilitate group video conferencing. These capacities include selective presentation of audio and, when in speaker view, enlarging the video of the one producing sound (presumably a person speaking, but could even be someone who accidently makes shuffling noises due to not muting a microphone) to dominate the screen. The Zoom bomb, as an aggressive relational phenomenon, is a technological intervention designed to bombard, attack, and literally disrupt the course of an engagement.[2] As such, the content, both visual and aural, associated with such bombs is meant to disturb and offend. Such interventions crack through the psychosocial milieu, re-forming it around its relational interruption.

Experiencing this, I am reminded of Claire Bishop's descriptions of Italian Futurist performances, or *serates,* of the early twentieth century. These events, which included painters, poets, and sculptors, were meant to offend the aesthetic sensibilities of the time, challenging their audiences through cacophonic and chaotic displays, which "usually included recitations of political statements and artistic manifestos, musical compositions, poetry, and painting," modelled on variety theatre (Bishop 2012, 41). The effect of these presentations was an instigation of chaos and antagonism, "with performers and audience making direct attacks on one another, frequently culminating in riot" (Bishop 2012, 45). Such an approach was aligned with the Futurists' aggressive ideological groundings that supported a drastic break with the past, embraced speed and

2. Christine Tran discusses how their PhD defense was Zoom bombed, raising significant points around gender, race, and consent in terms of such attacks (Tran 2021).

technology, and treated war as cleansing, later affiliated with Benito Mussolini and Italian fascism. The Futurists engaged with communications technologies, which at the time involved the mass printing of manifestos, flysheets, and press releases before and after *serates* to ensure that the event was promoted and documented. Bishop emphasizes the significance of this "conflation of the press, promotionalism, and politics" that were integral to these events. More than performance art, they became entanglements of artistic action with mass media technologies (Bishop 2012, 43).

I doubt that the Zoom bomb described above was instigated as an artwork (though considering the interventionist and shocking tactics of some performance artists, it is not beyond the realm of possibilities), and without a manifesto or explicit political agenda, like the Futurists, it is not possible to ascertain the exact motivations for such attacks. The utilization of shocking spectacles with technology, however, enables parallels to be drawn to these two types of disruption, albeit over 100 years apart. Considering the Zoom bomb as an aesthetic and ethical encounter, it is possible to become attuned to the relational capacities of livestreaming technology and the Zoom platform. The meeting I was attending has several precautions in place to preserve the integrity of the virtual space. It is a private meeting that requires a password, there is a waiting room for screening, and all people are muted upon arrival without the capacity to unmute unless enabled to do so by one of the hosts. However, with a meeting that has over 200 people, it is challenging to verify the intentions of all those who attend. This means that screening generally took place after admission and a disruption was made. In addition, the bomber, swarm of bombers, or perhaps tenacious few bombers (since the ability to switch Zoom accounts and names makes it impossible to confirm the number) had the capacity to unmute, which means they may have had access to hosting permissions. The ability to silence or eject a person as they speak or intervene in such a direct manner, through a technological click, is a possibility enabled in the virtual space. While processes of inclusion and exclusion are omnipresent to differing

degrees in social structures, the speed and effectiveness of muting
and blocking are something particular to the digital realm. Even
with such measures in place, the bomber(s) in this instance man-
aged to enter the meeting multiple times, with different names and
different tactics of disruption.

The disruption of the Zoom bomb not only draws attention to
the capacities of these technologies, but cultivates a disturbing
encounter of technologies and living beings. Simondon argues that
systems do not exist beyond an individual, but a milieu is constituted through individuation in conjunction with the individual.
Emphasis is placed on relation, which when applied to interpreting
livestreaming over the Internet highlights the connected nature of
the medium that is comprised of a distributed network. Relations
occur between individual human beings, but also through and with
technical objects, institutions, and other material and geographic
factors that comprise this milieu of Internet communication. In
addition, the webcam and microphone, as the primary tools used
for Internet broadcasting, are not reduced to determinist mediation
or simply lauded for the capacity to connect. Instead, these enable
a particular techno-aesthetic experience and are modified through
the relations of engagement that take place in these performances
of livestreaming. Here it becomes apparent how aesthetics is transformative but also entangled with ethics.

These encounters potentially instigate transduction through
engagement with technical objects. Transduction is a biological
and technological term Simondon uses to describe the process of
individuation within a domain. The example he uses to present
this process is crystallization, where solid forms emerge from a
supersaturated solution that exceed and carry the potential for
the crystals, while their creation is also tied to the environment
and conditions within which these processes take place. Technical
objects mediate, but as Brian Massumi observes, Simondon's definition of mediation differs from what is commonly used in communication studies, media studies, and cultural studies. Instead,
mediation "carries ontogenetic force, referring to a snapping into

relation effecting a self-inventive passing to a new level of existence" (Massumi 2012, 32). That is, mediation is not a means of control, but instead functions as a kind of bracketing or framing that influences processes of individuation through relation and co-constitution. These technologies alter how we engage with and relate to each other, inviting different forms of intimacy and interaction, but humans also alter the purpose of technical objects through engagement. These relational engagements are ongoing practices of connection between humans and nonhumans, where agencies comingle and clash.

The initial purpose of the discussed meeting was for people to come together as a collective with the intentions of supporting and taking care of each other with a shared purpose, with livestreaming technologies enabling and supporting such a gathering to occur. The format of the meeting and the means people engage with each other are working with the capacities of the technologies. The Zoom bomber(s), in contrast, present a counter purpose with the intention of disrupting the gathering. The tensions that arise from conflicting agencies reveal an ethics of care that is an ongoing process of interaction, as designated individuals work to remove the disrupters. Technological systems act as mediators of the meeting, with technologies both enabling disruption and its cessation. In this context, the implications of care seem straightforward: the bomber(s) are in the wrong and must be removed as soon as possible. However, such moralistic solutions risk reducing the ethical considerations of technology, where the technological capacities to block the bomber(s) with the click of a mouse have the capacity to restrict other users, thereby potentially countering the collective's shared purpose. Such relations are situated within the context of material engagement, including technological systems that make such engagements possible. Drawing attention to these ethical implications moves away from a generic understanding of care, which according to Puig de la Bellacasa, thickens its meaning and emphasizes its ongoing relationality, ambivalent complexities, and "situated implications" (Puig de la Bellacasa

2017, 24). In the following section, I apply this approach to the activities of camgirls of the 1990s as a first generation of Internet broadcasters who helped define the medium through their practice yet are often undervalued or discredited as being simply self-objectifying exhibitionists.

Glitch, Noise, and Techno-Grrrls

DURING THE 1990S AND EARLY 2000S, when Internet connections became more common in households along with the increased proliferation of personal computers, a number of women began setting up webcams and broadcasting their activities over the Internet. Some of these women gained popular followings and established a means of income. Referred to as "camgirls," these women engaged in lifecasting (Senft 2008). The descriptor camgirl refers to the fact that this early group of Internet broadcasters were predominantly cisgender women. Still photographs were uploaded from webcams, which during the 1990s, refreshed every few minutes due to the restricted capacity of the Internet to upload files at that time. Even though these early broadcasts involved silent, still images uploaded minutes apart, this practice is an antecedent for video streaming that arose a little over a decade later and anticipates present-day social media platforms. Since these camgirls worked prior to the advent of Web 2.0, when private, corporate social media platforms facilitated the capacity to share webcam imagery online, many developed skills in web design and development, including HTML and CSS, to produce their webcam sites. The first woman recognized for popularizing this engagement with the webcam is Jennifer Ringley, who set up "Jennicam" in 1996 in her college dorm room. Another camgirl, Ana Voog, established a unique online presence through creative engagement with technological limitations as networked experiments, creating spaces online as she attempted to challenge patriarchal norms of gender and sexuality through performance art. In contrast to certain analyses of camgirls, particularly those that emphasize the countering of the white "male gaze" as the main source of resistance, I treat this broadcasting of the self as a type of durational digital performance art and the aesthetics of this digital performance resulting from technological engagement, with particular attention to glitch and noise.

Webcamming as Art

Ana Voog is one of the early camgirls recognized for her contributions to the medium, cultivating a distinctive style and performance practice in relation to the camera. Anacam was one of the longest running webcam sites, at thirteen years, starting in 1997 and ending in 2009. On an archived version of Voog's website, it is possible to watch a stream of images. These can be played back at a refresh rate of 600 seconds, or a faster rate of thirty seconds.[1] They can also be viewed in the order they were shot or at random. There is an option to jump to specific frames, though some of the archived images do not load properly. Watching this stream of images in 2020, after becoming acclimated to the immediacy of livestreaming video and radically decreased online response times, even the thirty-second refresh rate involves a test of patience.

Voog's presence ranges from the documentation of mundane activities to playful interventions. In one series of shots, Voog appears to be playing with a graphic of a colored circle on the screen. Even though these images are taken minutes apart, when played in quick succession they take on an animated effect, with Voog behaving as if the digital circle is an orb or ball that she can manipulate with her hands. A simple gestural performance, this sequence

---

1. The archived version of her site can be accessed at http://anavoog. com/anacam.com/anaframesn.html.

highlights how Voog is aware of the camera, her body, and resulting digital image as an artistic medium and performance site through the screen. Images are taken from various angles: some close-up while others are shot from a high corner of the room, like a CCTV security camera. It was not uncommon for Voog to appear naked. In some images, Voog posed directly for the camera provocatively and engaged in sexual activities, while in other instances she treats her state of undress with the same comfort of wearing clothes. Cameras were on 24/7, capturing a feed of her life as it unfolded not on camera, but *with* the cameras as a durational performance where Voog cultivated a milieu through her growing following on the Internet, with her site receiving millions of visits per day during the late 1990s (Knight 2000).

In addition to showing herself and her daily activities, Voog pointed the camera at objects around her apartment that she found interesting, sometimes adding text and colored effects to the images. At the top of all broadcast images is a phrase created through a random word generator, a digital Dada poem. The images are low resolution, though their noisy quality contribute to a style that Voog cultivates. In certain respects, the work is evocative of that of Cindy Sherman, as she is performing for and with the camera, turning the image into an exploratory space of femme identity that plays with and challenges presentations of gender and sexuality through a "performance art persona" (Senft 2008, 26). Voog is conscientious about her playfulness with the medium and performance-based approach: "I was the seventh camgirl, and the first to call webcamming art!" (as quoted in Senft 2008, 39). Voog is not just posing for the camera, but treats it as part of the performance itself. Emma Maguire observes how Voog uses her body as "*media*—as a malleable, formable, shapeable material with which to make her art. The webcam, too, is media, and her work is an exploration of the effects of bringing these two mediums—one flesh, the other a digital machine—together" (Maguire 2018, 41). Treating the body as medium is a standard feature of performance art. Voog's images have a staged quality to them that border on theatrical, enhanced by her strained positioning of the head, twisting up of the body, or awareness of her gaze and that of her viewer. In many of the images, Voog is looking to the side and toward the computer monitor, pointing to her awareness of how an image is composed. She also regularly uses mirrors as a prop, drawing attention to the presence of the camera as she performs with it, reflecting it back into the image frame of the screen.

Techno-Grrrls

The term "camgirl" warrants further discussion. Ringley and others, including Teresa Senft (2008) who both studied camgirls and hosted her own webcam site, use this term to refer to their broadcasting activities. Michelle White argues against using it, instead referring to them as women webcam operators, since she argues the term camgirl is infantilizing and eroticizing, downplaying the "women webcam operators' complex skills" (White 2003, 15). As Maguire notes, instead of treating Jennifer Ringley as "innovative" or a "tech pioneer" in her novel approach to engaging with the webcam, she is dismissed as a "novelty" and "exhibitionist" (Maguire 2018, 35). However, Maguire continues to use the term "camgirl" as a provocation. The term "girl" does not need to be treated as infantilizing, but is part of a broader trend of the late twentieth century where women claimed the term as a source of empowerment, most notably in punk rock through the Riot Grrrl feminist network (Leonard 2017). Maguire describes how the term girl "broadly denotes a gendered identity that signifies both youth and femininity (although not necessarily femaleness) as distinct from mature womanhood" (Maguire 2018, 6). That is, girlhood is not restricted to a particular age bracket, but used to identify a process of subjective becoming. In the context of this book, the term girl is consistent with the spirit of Riot Grrrl, where youth subcultures embraced feminine contributions as a means of feminist gender rebellion. Senft (2008) highlights how the personal-as-political, feminist response of Riot Grrrl to the marginalization of women in punk and indie rock cultures can be found in the confessional quality of 1990s cam girls. However, I extend this observation to consider how these women engaged with technologies. Just as Riot Grrrl critiqued the masculinist culture of punk and indie rock music through DIY practice, camgirls challenged the masculinist hacker culture of the tech industry as Techno-grrrls. I want to reiterate that even though many early camgirls were cisgender women, I do not consider the term girl as innately connected to biological femaleness. Rather, it evokes a certain performance of youthful femininity that is not determined by biological sex or assigned gender.

From Empowerment to Encounters

Current aesthetic analyses of camgirls emphasize empowerment with a focus on women's control over the production and distribution of the image, which contrasted from mainstream media (Knight 2000; Maguire 2018; Senft 2008; White 2003; 2006). In particular, there is a desire to invert the subject/object binary. That is, while men have typically been treated as the subject (the looker) and women as the object (to-be-looked-at in the language of film theorist Laura Mulvey), this binary can be inverted where the art object as female looks back, making the male subject/ viewer uncomfortable. Michelle White uses this approach in her analysis of women webcam operators, arguing that the spectator's gaze is "too close to see" (White 2003, 20). She maintains that the computer screen, unlike the film screen, is one where the viewer and subject are positioned closely to the monitor, with images uploaded and displayed minutes apart with regular technical glitches. The result is a display of images that is fractured where the spectator is too proprioceptively close compared to the "classic viewing position" of cinema.

Focusing solely on empowerment, however, is restrictive as it limits the subversive capacity through the ability to frame the image and to look back, even as an aesthetics of inversion. In addition to placing focus on the masculine consumer as the beholder of the gaze, this approach generalizes gender based on the experiences of white women, excluding and at the expense of Black women and women of color. Aria Dean problematizes this obsession with the male gaze that persists through twenty-first century selfie artists. These qualities are also found as a prominent theme in the work of feminist artists who work with social media platforms, such as Ann Hirsch and Amalia Ulmann, who attempt to reveal the constructs of this gaze through performed avatars of white cisgender femininity. Dean describes how white, cisgender, nondisabled, female identifying artists praise the challenge to the gaze capacity of the selfie as "*the primary* feminist tool for resistance [. . .] follow[ing] a logic in which the circulation of personal narratives through Instagram and other social media platforms is supposed to provide points of identification for all women" (A. Dean 2016). Anticipating the rise of social media, camgirls popularized the Internet as a platform for producing and sharing autobiographical narratives through images. Camgirl culture of the 1990s and 2000s included predominately young, white, cisgender women. Through webcams, these women opened up their domestic spaces and lives to the public space of the Internet. While these women have challenged gender norms through their digital performances, such performances relate to a particular kind of femme-ness that is marked as white. As Legacy Russell points out in relation to cyberfeminism, "hypervisibility of white faces and voices across feminist cyberculture demonstrated ongoing exclusion, even within this new, 'utopic' setting" (Russell 2020, 33). These qualities exist in Victor Burgin's critical reading of Jennifer Ringley's performances, where he infantilizes her and "rescues" her from criticisms of exhibitionism. Burgin argues that Ringley is merely a girl finding her way in the world: "Parading around her websited dorm room in spike heels, Jenni is tottering around in her mother's shoes. Under the gaze of her mother she is investigating what it is to be a woman, like her mother" (Burgin 2000, 85). Despite the fact Ringley was twenty-one at that time and legally recognized as an adult, Burgin insists on her "fledgling sexuality." His persistent claims of her innocence, however, are possible due to her unacknowledged whiteness, where white, youthful, cis, female heterosexuality is assumed to be inherently virtuous as "white women's whiteness can always help them find their way back to respectability" (Hamad 2020, 75). Any displays otherwise are dismissed as a "child . . . recklessly launch[ing] itself into the void" under the protective gaze of her mother (Burgin 2000, 84).

Thus, I take a different approach to analyzing the practice of camgirls, without making universal claims of empowerment. Rather, I frame it as aesthetic and ethical encounters with a focus on technical objects and, like Voog, a work of performance art. Lifecasting functions as what Brooke Knight describes camming as: a "never-ending nonevent" (Knight 2000, 25). While Voog indicates how she began camming as a way to explain or present herself and create "at all times" (Krotoski 2016), what actually was presented on the screen was fractured documentation of various gestures and activities. For instance, when Voog pointed the camera at different scenes or objects in her apartment that seemed interesting, with these shots uploaded every few minutes, they didn't always make sense. It is these moments of obfuscation and confusion that intrigue me, where attention is not placed on visibility, but on abstracting the image in a playful way. The performed actions in these early days of Internet broadcasting are provocative, before they became codified, tracked, and nudged through the infiltrative infrastructures of what is referred to as surveillance capitalism (Zuboff 2019), the attention economy (Citton 2017; Wu 2016), or as McKenzie Wark (2019) speculates, perhaps capitalism is dead and this is something worse. My interest here is not so much in the content of the performances, but the unique encounters that emerge through the relational mediation of the web camera, Internet, and computer monitor.

The aesthetics of camgirls' broadcasted images were influenced by the material qualities of the technologies, including slow modem speeds and low camera resolution. Here, the webcam is not just a capture device, the Internet is not just a telecommunications network, and the computer monitor is not just a machine for display; but these constitute what Simondon refers to as technical

objects. As noted in the introduction, he does not consider technology merely a vehicle for human activity or tools at our disposal.
Simondon argues that technical objects function as part of a milieu
that they modify, thereby making technology, humans, and their
surrounding environment co-constitutive. The range of technologies that camgirls of this period used, including the webcam, self-
maintained websites, FTP servers, archives with limited storage
space, dial-up modems, and chat rooms, helped inform how these
technologies are relational, as the camgirls adopted and modified
them. Technical objects, for Simondon (2016), are not restricted to
particular uses, but also have a degree of indeterminacy that invite
other, even unanticipated actions. This indeterminacy means that
even though technical objects have material properties that invite
specific gestures, they may also be repurposed and used in ways that
are not intended. Such engagement of technology anticipates the
Maker movement that Silicon Valley promotes as a phenomenon of
innovation, but it also connects to longer histories of technological
modification through necessity, or what Nettrice Gaskins (2019;
2021) refers to as techno-vernacular creativity (TVC): the informal
engagement of science and technology by underrepresented ethnic
groups, including African diaspora, Latinx, and Indigenous groups
in the United States, through communities of practice in local contexts. Gaskin states: "Do-it-yourself or maker culture—creating
technology without expert input—is a newer contribution to this
age-old, global practice and, in some cases, make use of TVC modes/
methods" (Gaskins 2019, 255), which include re-appropriation,
improvisation, and conceptual remixing. The hacking and modification practices of camgirls involve TVC methods, though their
technological innovations are commonly dismissed as frivolous in
a gesture of techno-sexism.

In short, many camgirls were required to create their own websites and provide their own broadcasting capacities, as streaming
platforms such as Justin.tv were not yet available. Internet capacities at the time also influenced production, as the cost of bandwidth
was variable and unpredictable, depending on the amount of infor-

mation that was transmitted to end users. That is, as more people visited the site, the amount of data that was transferred increased. Rising popularity of a camgirl's website made it more expensive for the camgirl to produce (Senft 2008). Internet connectivity was also limited in terms of data transfer, as most connections at the time involved telephone modems, with access to DSL and Broadband only arriving in the 2000s. As a result of these technological factors, broadcast images were full of gaps, noise, glitch, and breakdown.

The Aesthetics of Glitch and Maintenance as Care

Art historian Carolyn Kane defines glitch as "a problematic, annoying, or unintended error that, like the definition of error, tends to be negligible, quickly absorbed by the larger, still-functioning system" (Kane 2019, 15). She observes how the glitch has given rise to its own genre of art at the end of the twentieth century—simultaneously the time of first-generation camgirls. However, for camgirls, the glitch was not the "fodder for a new style of art-making" (Kane 2019, 15). Instead, glitch was an inevitable quality of livestreaming that typically emerged from a breakdown of these DIY broadcasts. Kane provides a considered aesthetic analysis of the glitch, tying it to a longer history of visual noise and chromatic aberrations found in abstract expressionism and other modernist art, as well as notions of failure and breakdown in Western philosophy. Kane argues that the glitch, along with error, failure, noise, and trash, are not anomalies against an ongoing progressive stride toward perfection, but instead, the often unacknowledged norm of certain breakdown. Glitches, as aesthetic manifestations of failure, are everywhere despite ongoing attempts at denial in Western philosophy, art, and media.

While Simondon does not specifically reference the "glitch," he does acknowledge noise in his discussion of aesthetics. In *On the Mode of Existence of Technical Objects*, Simondon describes a telephone center as an aesthetic experience, arguing that the white noise that accompanies communication throughout these channels is not to be ignored for the "meaningful signal," but integral to the technological system that makes such communication possible (Simondon 2016, 198). Simondon states that the aesthetic experience emerges from the *intention* to communicate. The noise that accompanies communication does not need to be treated as an unwelcome disruption, but is integral to our engagement with technical objects, and therefore part of its techno-aesthetics. Like the audible noise that accompanies early long-distance telephone calls, the glitches and other visual manifestations of breakdown that comprise the imagery of first-generation camgirls are indicators of a desire to communicate, part of the broader systems that make such communications possible. In Voog's broadcast images, sometimes these glitches are manifest as silvery, cubic swatches, consuming chunks of images that do not transmit properly. Noise is also present in the colorful visual artifacts of image compression, unavoidable during the 1990s and early 2000s when limited technological capacities meant low camera resolutions and inhibited the sharing of large files.

The aesthetic qualities that result from technological limitations should not be dismissed merely as errors, despite the frustrations that arise from breakdown, ranging from glitched images and broken links to more significant website malfunctions that disrupt service. Voog comments upon such disruptions in her streamed images, describing her efforts to maintain her site's functionality. Here she draws attention to the breakdowns—the glitches and noise—which are not edited out but comprise part of the broader stream. These qualities make the desire to communicate evident through the work, as the influence of the webcam and Internet on Voog's actions as technical objects are apparent. Her labor is made visible, with these acts of technological maintenance functioning as gestures of care (Puig de la Bellacasa 2017). Voog is engaging in what Lucy Suchman refers to as situated actions, "actions taken in context of particular, concrete circumstances" (Suchman 2007, 26). The glitch functions as an aesthetic manifestation of such care ethics, which influence not only the technological systems, but the collective that Voog has formed around her webcasting. This collective involves the individuation of individuals, including living humans and nonliving technical objects, but also comprises processes of transindividuation, or shared experiences of individuation that exceed individuals. Individuation and transindividuation are not distinct processes, but interconnected. Transindividuation, for Simondon (2020), is not simply harmonious. As he reiterates throughout his philosophy, it involves transduction and becoming that include potentials of the pre-individual and states of metastability, as well as expectations and tensions from various involved individuals. The technical glitch and its resolution are one such tension of agencies between human and machine in this realized ethics of care as maintenance.

Therefore, the technology of camming influenced the quality of the imagery produced, cultivating distinctive stylistics connected to its limitations. In addition to the visual qualities discussed above, there were also gaps between images. These gaps have been commented upon by various writers and scholars, including Voog herself. She notes how her viewers would project stories onto the image sequences that did not accurately convey what was happening in the images as a kind of digital Rorschach Test (Krotoski 2016). As such, the aesthetic qualities of Voog's camming practice are informed through her engagement with technology, or its techno-aesthetics. As noted in the introduction, Simondon emphasizes how techno-aesthetics is not focused on contemplation, but "it's in usage, in action, that it becomes something orgasmic, a tactile means and motor of stimulation" (Simondon 2012, 3). Simondon's use of sexual language is notable here, especially when considered in relation to camgirls where the pornographic has been used as a means of dismissing their activities. In techno-aesthetics, Simondon focuses on how engagement with tools and machines, particularly in nonart contexts that tend not to be treated as aesthetic, evokes aesthetic sensations: "When a nut that is stuck becomes unstuck, one experiences a motoric pleasure, a certain instrumentalized joy, a communication—mediated by the tool—with the thing on which the tool is working" (Simondon 2012, 3). In particular, Simondon focuses on how human bodies and technical objects work in tandem, where "the body of the operator gives and receives" (Simondon 2012, 3). Unlike other philosophers of aesthetics, Simondon is not only interested in the impact of an art object once it is produced, but treats the process of creation as a type of aesthetic experience:

> Art is not only the object of contemplation; for those who practice it, it's a form of action [. . .] Aesthetics is not only, nor first and foremost, the sensation of the "consumer" of the work of art. It is also, and more originally so, the set of sensations, more or less rich, of the artists themselves: it's about a certain contact with matter that is being transformed through work (Simondon 2012, 3).

The aesthetic, for Simondon, is not specific to the art object, but "it is the encounter—which takes place about the object—between a real aspect of the world and a human gesture" (Simondon 2016, 202). Even though Voog's camming practice through Anacam has ended, the project as a whole encompassed thirteen years of working with various technical objects to produce and maintain the cam feeds and site—thirteen years of process that were co-constituted as performance, aesthetic, and ethical encounters while being produced. Voog was not just producing Anacam; Anacam was also constituting Voog. Both were cultivating an online network that contributed to the growth of an online community, which at its height involved millions of visits to the site.

Since first-generation camgirls were working prior to social media platforms that have normalized many of these lifecasting activities, there was not a template for such production at that time. As women designed and programmed their sites, they also established methods for connecting along with developing the techno-aesthetics of the resulting encounters with the site through maintenance as an ethics of care. In addition to sharing images uploaded from webcams and coding websites, camgirls set up chat rooms, online shops, archives of images, and blogs in order to engage with a growing following of fans from around the world. This milieu consists of the camgirls and the technical objects used to produce the sites, but also the geographic space of their homes as the setting of their camming work and the millions of individuals connected as part of the network that arose around their sites. Observing images archived on Voog's site that have been shot over the years, evidence of change can be found throughout. Her engagement with the camera alters over time, as her actions indicate a process of artistic experimentation. Improved capacities of cameras enabled increased resolution of images, but also the website was modified as Internet affordances improved, such as the introduction of DSL. These processes of change encompass what Simondon refers to as individuation and transindividuation. With Anacam, individuation does not just occur through Voog's processes of subjective becoming in conjunction with her technical objects. The technical objects also individuate as these are modified or replaced with newer versions. Change occurs through the iterative progression of transduction. Simondon emphasizes the significance of relations involved in these processes, where change is biological, physical, but also social through the growth of a networked collective. Individuation of physical and vital beings occurs through the techno-aesthetics of these first generation camgirls, where such processes are co-constitutive and transindividuating through a relational ethics of care as becoming.

Aesthetics of Duration and Transformative Justice

DURING LATE MAY 2020, I was speaking over Zoom with some-one in Vermont as I sat in my home office in Ireland. She informed me that she had been watching livestreams from protests in Minneapolis on the nonprofit independent media platform Unicorn Riot. She described the intensity of events unfolding in the streets of this Minnesota city, which emerged in response to a video of officer Derek Chauvin murdering George Floyd that went viral on social media earlier that week. At this stage, coverage of these events over major media networks was limited. Livestreams of these protests became a significant means of witnessing while geographic movements were confined through social distancing due to the Covid-19 pandemic. Shortly thereafter, Black Lives Matter protests and marches began to take place around the United States and world, including a march in Dublin during early June, many of which were livestreamed over social media. Leslie Alexander and Michelle Alexander describe how this summer involved "the largest racial-justice protests in history—including people of all colors and ages and from all walks of life," indicating a shift in the historical cycle of racist violence and social response (Alexander and Alexander 2021, 121).

Livestreaming and Social Movements

Livestreaming has played an increasingly significant role in trans-
formative justice movements since 2011, including the Occupy
movement, 15M in Spain (Kavada and Treré 2020), the Quebec
Student Strike (Thorburn 2014), the Native American led Anti-
Dakota Access Pipeline (NO DAPL) movement in the Standing Rock
Sioux reservation in North Dakota (Martini 2018), and Black Lives
Matter (Kumanyika 2017). Once livestreaming was more accessible through platforms such as Twitch, YouTube, Facebook, and
Periscope/Twitter, it became an important strategy in resistance
activities, including inviting virtual witnesses and building networks of support without relying on major news networks and
mainstream journalism for coverage. Livestreaming is part of what
Sasha Costanza-Chock refers to as social movement media cultures,
or the "set of tools, skills, social practices and norms that movement participants deploy to create, circulate, curate and amplify
movement media across all available platforms" (Costanza-Chock
2012, 375). Traditional activist strategies and analogue media, including print-based formats such as posters and leaflets, merge with
digital technological development and engagement. Scholars and
activists who highlight the growing importance of livestreaming in
social-justice movements tend to emphasize the impact of streaming
on the development of activists (including those on-the-ground,
streamers, and witnesses of streams) as subjects. Overall, there is
a certain degree of ambivalence relating to the impact of streaming
on activism, though generally such technologies are promoted for
their capacity to engage with the unpredictability of social justice
and invite new modes of participation for activists. Instead of focusing on the implications of livestreaming from an activist or citizen
journalist perspective, I want to consider this media as aesthetic
encounter, which is also a political and ethical encounter, just as it
is a relational experience of transindividuation.

Simondon emphasizes how the living being is not self-contained,
but is comprised of an interior milieu that is relative to an exterior

milieu. Individuation, therefore, is relative, which includes relations to other physical and living beings. Referencing Spinoza and the human's recognition of fragility, Simondon states:

> Facing natural life, we feel that we are as perishable as the leaves of a tree; within us, the aging of the being that passes makes tangible the precariousness that responds to this upsurge, this emergence of life radiating in other beings; the ways are diverse in the paths of life, and we intersect with other beings of all ages that are themselves in all periods of life (Simondon 2020, 277).

Individuation comprises the psychological as well as the social, with society presenting "a network of states and of roles through which individual behavior must pass" (Simondon 2020, 327). The social informs the becoming of individuals, though in turn, individuals impact the social through relation and rapport. Simondon describes transindividuation as not simply individuating together, or inter-individuation, but connects to "how the living being lives at the limit of itself, on its limit" (Simondon 2020, 251). Transindividuation involves the existence of individuals together within the social milieu as we come to the limits of our individual being, containing "potentials and metastability, expectation and tension, the discovery of a structure and of a functional organization" (Simondon 2020, 339). Elizabeth Grosz highlights the significance of Simondon's thinking for "feminist, anti-racist and radical political thought," as he "opens up new ways of understanding identity transformation and creation—all central ingredients in a radical reconceptualization of thought" (Grosz 2012, 37). This is the framing of Simondon's relational ethics and politics of becoming, which are also aesthetic. Jacques Rancière argues that aesthetics does not simply move people to political action, but aesthetics is political, as aesthetic acts are "configurations of experience that create new modes of sense perception and induce novel forms of political subjectivity" (Rancière 2014, 3). Livestreaming in social-justice movements, moreover, is not just political, but as moving image works that involve the sharing of the sensible, such streams are also aesthetic even though these streams are not created as art. In order to make the relationship between the political and the aesthetic more explicit, I complement Simondon's techno-aesthetics with Rancière's definition of aesthetics as "a mode of articulation between ways of doing and making, their corresponding forms of visibility, and possible ways of thinking about their relationships" (Rancière 2014, 4). The techno-aesthetics of livestreaming, therefore, are what makes the political possible, as politics "revolves around what is seen and what can be said about it, around who has the ability to see and the talent to speak, around the properties of spaces and the possibilities of time" (Rancière 2014, 8).

Of all the recent movements to engage with livestreaming, Black Lives Matter has gained significant traction globally since it began in 2014 and has become the visible forefront of racial justice activism currently in the United States. Livestreaming and digital technologies have long played a significant role in the movement, even prior to the massive uptake of streaming during 2020. Charlton McIlwain (2020) describes how social media and web-based digital tools were integral to the rise and growth of Black Lives Matter, which began as a social media post, connecting the movement to a longer history of computation supporting racial justice movements and Black community building. Chenjerai Kumanyika (2017) discusses the significance of livestreaming in Black Lives Matter protests as a digital native, networked movement. Drawing from his experiences of streaming Black Lives Matter actions and viewing events and protests online, Kumanyika highlights the technical and aesthetic features of livestreaming social-justice activities, with emphasis on how these contrast from traditional media channels while being entwined with the changing needs and logistics of resistance movements today. Kumanyika's account of streaming not only provides a conceptual understanding of its significance, but he centers the physical and technological aspects of broadcasting over the Internet. The embodied and phenomenological characteristics of streaming social-justice actions emphasize how the aesthetic qualities of streaming extend beyond the images produced, but include the relational gestures of creators, on-the-ground activists, virtual audiences, and others involved in the production, consumption, and impact of these broadcasts. These features enable an understanding of the supports needed to make livestreaming possible, thus contributing to livestreaming's techno-aesthetics, as well as the impact that technology has on the body while mediating the stream online.

From Representation to Aesthetic Encounter

While today's social-justice livestreams are not generally considered art works or performances by their creators, they are aesthetic encounters through the production and sharing of video within the realm of political activism off- and online. Engagement with technology in social movements creates the techno-geographic milieu within which activism occurs. According to Simondon (2016), this is also the relational context within which technical objects exist, informing and situating the technical being. For instance, Kumanyika discusses technological considerations of mobile livestreaming, such as carrying a portable USB charger to prolong battery life as well as ensuring that data plans and mobile phone coverage enable and support streaming. The technical needs of streaming directly impact activities on the ground, and also impact the person streaming. Kumanyika notes how "frequently walking long distances with marching protesters can be demanding. These challenges include the physical work of holding the phone—often with arms raised for several hours" (Kumanyika 2017, 176). Streamers may provide editorial commentary, verbally describing what is happening, which offers information about an event, but also counters the potential boredom of long, unedited takes. Some streamers respond directly to comments from the virtual audience in chat features, though the delay in timing between posting a text comment, having it become visible, and then reading by the streamer indicates how these interactions are not immediate. The act of streaming, therefore, can be considered a durational digital performance where the streamer is not an objective observer, but integrated into the techno-geographic milieu of protest both on-the-ground and virtually.

At the same time, as with the camgirls, technologies influence the style of the stream. While initially streams may have been shot in the horizontal or landscape format that has been the standard for moving image since the invention of the film camera, increasingly streams have been shot in the vertical or portrait style as the capacity to stream with smartphones has become more accessible and affordable, including the ability to transmit large quantities of data over cellular networks and major social media platforms, like Instagram, designed to accommodate this framing. Other stylistic qualities include long durational shots where not much happens, with the streamer staying still as action unfolds (again, evocative of more traditional film aesthetics) or moving with the smartphone as a handheld device, with these movements visible through the shaking of the frame. In order to minimize such movements, gimbles or camera stabilizers are now designed specifically for smartphones, making the camera a more fluid extension of the body. In addition, there is a slight delay between action as it unfolds on the ground and online, evident for example when streamers verbally respond to viewers' typed comments as noted above. This delay or lag, like glitch and noise, is indicative of technical objects, drawing their mediating presence to the fore, which I define as the digital aesthetics of interruption (Putnam 2022).

These are just some of the stylistic qualities of activist livestreaming, but aesthetics is not just descriptors of experiencing a work of art or media. Rather, aesthetics involves the sharing of the sensible—a means of relating to others through sensation. Such experiences may involve formal qualities and style, though aesthetics is not limited simply to these features. Instead, aesthetics has a broader sense, as described by Bernard Stiegler, "where *aisthēsis* means sensory perception, and where the question of aesthetics is, therefore that of feeling and sensibility in general" (Stiegler 2014, 1). These sensations are not restricted to art per se, though art has tended to take priority in aesthetics, despite the fact that "art as a notion designating a specific form of experience has only existed in the West since the end of the eighteenth century" (Rancière 2019, lx). When extending the scope of aesthetics beyond art, it is possible to consider the capacity of livestreaming beyond content or journalistic narrative. Aesthetics, as the sharing of the sensible, provides an affective experience that exceeds quantification and enables us to inquire into the unknown. Aesthetics enables considerations of the capacity to relate to the sensibilities of others and the intention of social movements to build a political community through feeling together. These affective relations introduce perception through the sharing of sensation, which Simondon (2020) describes as informing how subjects relate to the world. For social-justice movements, this sharing of the sensible is political: it can build support through affective encounters of moving image. At the same time, the technologies of streaming are not merely neutral platforms; they are also ethical because they are entangled with and mediate how these aesthetic encounters manifest. These technologies bridge geographic distance, but also influence how time is experienced.

Cross Section of Time and Aesthetics of Duration

Something was different in 2020. There was increased attunement through virtual connections due to being apart physically. Even though social media and livestreaming were already recognized staples of communication, they became our vital tethers to each other. It is difficult to fully grasp the impact of this shift, even in 2023 (as I finish this book) as societies are transitioning to a different state of living (and dying) with the virus. adrienne maree brown describes the impact of the pandemic on our emotional states: "we are stuck in our houses or endangering ourselves to go out and work, terrified and angry at the loss of our plans and normalcy [. . .]. Grieving our unnecessary dead, many of whom are dying alone, unheld by us. We are full of justified rage. And we want to release that rage" (brown 2020, 24). brown considers how this emotional shift has become manifest in an increase in callouts and takedowns, or collective and public ways of bringing pressure onto organizations and individuals, concerning abuses of power, on the behalf of minoritized and oppressed individuals and groups. Jodi Dean (2010) describes how digital subjects are caught in endless loops of reflexivity, which are evident in the feeding frenzies brown identifies as affiliated with the detrimental callouts occurring within social-justice movements. brown has noted how through social media and digital networks "our access to the global scale of suffering has become immediate, through technology, but we have not developed the capacity to be with that increased awareness of suffering" (brown 2017, 149). Dean refers to this increased transmission of emotion as the circulation of affect, "as networks generate and amplify spectacular effects" (J. Dean 2010, 29). The Covid-19 pandemic exasperated what has already been present in these technological networks, as individuals are transformed through technological engagement with other individuals, both human and physical.

It is within this context that the Black Lives Matter protests and other anti-racist, social-justice actions took place in 2020, with livestreaming offering a quality of immediacy and contact during a time of geographic and physical separation. However, the capacities to relate, even affectively, have been invariably different, which include experiences of time. Commenting upon engagement with social media in social-justice work, brown states: "Real time is slower than social media time, where everything feels urgent. Real time often includes periods of silence, reflection, growth, space, self-forgiveness, processing with loved ones, rest, and responsibility" (brown 2017, 110). Such urgency became intensified during the Covid-19 pandemic, with social media being a significant means to connect with others. Periods of healing and rest increasingly metamorphasized into digital forms. In contrast, livestreaming introduces distinct ways of experiencing time over social media.

Social media typically involves rapid consumption of content, scanned through endless scrolling. Livestreams, however, involve a different presentation of time. During streams, especially the streams of events such as protests and other social-justice actions, there is always the possibility of *something* happening. Generally, these livestreams are presented in anticipation of something occurring, usually involving the camera operator streaming for multiple hours, which is longer than standard media productions. Kumanyika refers to streams as "slow media," which for online witnesses cultivates a "shared sense of virtual presence with the streamer and with the protestors" (Kumanyika 2017, 180). Unlike certain live broadcasts where there is a synchronized unfolding of activity, like a choreographed performance such as Yara Travieso's 2017 livestreamed dance film *La Medea* (see Putnam 2022), with streaming at activist events the camera just rolls. That is, the camera is on and the streamer presents for prolonged periods. Livestreaming, therefore, introduces a different scale of time in the realms of virtual and "real-world" time that brown discusses, pointing to another means of relating temporally through digital technologies.

Livestreaming, as a form of DIY internet broadcast, invites an aesthetic experience of duration for both the streamer and the viewer, where emphasis is not necessarily placed on the unfolding of action as it happens, but the potential that something *might* happen. Performance studies scholar Adrian Heathfield defines aesthetic duration, drawing from the philosophy of Henri Bergson, as a means of "dealing in the confusion of temporal distinctions [. . .] drawing the spectator into the thick braids of paradoxical times" (Hsieh and Heathfield 2015, 22). The aesthetics of duration are not just visual; they are experienced through the body of the creator and the viewer, enabling recognition of time's structure while exceeding the framing of these structures. These aesthetic qualities of activist livestreams are evocative of slow cinema, which emerged during the twentieth century in contrast to the quick pace of mainstream filmmaking that compresses narrative and stimulates attention in two- to three-hour blocks.

Matthew Flanagan describes how slow cinema is characterized by "the employment of (often extremely) long takes, de-centered and understated modes of storytelling, and a pronounced emphasis on quietude and the everyday" (Flanagan 2008). Such qualities are evident in works such as Andy Warhol's *Sleep* (1964) and *Empire* (1965). *Sleep* consists of looped footage of Warhol's lover at the time, John Giorno, sleeping, while *Empire* is comprised of slow-motion footage of New York City's iconic Empire State Building illuminated at night. These avant-garde works counter the stylistic norms of mainstream filmmaking, not just in their excessive running lengths (five hours and twenty minutes for *Sleep* and eight hours and five minutes for *Empire*), but also the presence of very minimal activity and lack of narrative arc. Activist livestreams also involve extremely long takes, unedited and shared synchronously while being shot, and do not have the narrative structure of mainstream media presentations. Unlike Warhol's productions, the streamer may act as a narrator of events in order to provide clarity for virtual audiences and encourage engagement, sometimes responding directly to online viewers. These qualities also differ from traditional journalist media, where the streamer as reporter directly engages with the virtual audience, but there is a lack of editing between the streamer's footage and cuts to a news station anchor, as is common with televised journalism. Slowness in this context, according to Rancière (2016), is not just aesthetic, but also political in its engagement with the materiality of time. Time is presented as time unfolds, where the phenomenology of the stream cultivates an aesthetic experience of time that is consistent with the pace of time for the streamer. Time is also politicized through social-justice action on the ground and online.

However, there are differences in the aesthetic experience of duration in livestreaming from gallery performances and slow cinema, particularly in the capacities of the viewer to engage with media through the affordances of technology. When witnessing a durational work in the context of a gallery or a cinema, the viewer is invited to engage with the work in a concentrated state of attention, as distractions are minimized through the framing of the work in the white cube or darkened theatre. Natalie Loveless describes how "durational performance that asks its audience to *be there* without

giving the members of that audience anything to do or be distract-
ed by (either in the form of expressed affect, implied narrative, or
verbal language) is not a familiar literacy for many" (Loveless 2013,
131). Such types of witnessing "demand quiet attention and presence
for an invested length of time during which there is little happening," which involve an endurance for both the artist and audience
(Loveless 2013, 132). In contrast, with activist livestreaming, the
streamer may be engaged in this type of durational performance,
though the experiences of virtual witnesses differ due to the capacities and affordances of social media interfaces that enable what
Katherine Hayles describes as hyper attention, which is "characterized by switching focus rapidly among different tasks, preferring
multiple information streams, seeking a high level of stimulation,
and having a low tolerance for boredom" (Hayles 2007, 187). When
viewing a video online, interface design invites switching between
different tasks. A video may be open in a separate window or tab on
a computer desktop or can be presented in the foreground of the
desktop when in picture-in-picture mode. Such features are also
present on mobile devices, with the ability to watch a stream as a
minimized window at the foreground of the screen while continuing to scroll through a social media feed. Even if a video is open in
a window, there is also not a guarantee that the viewer is actually
watching the content in a focused manner. The nonlinear design
of graphic user interfaces does not just invite switch tasking, but
fosters it through technological affordances.

This type of engagement with internet broadcasting is not new
to more recent social media platforms, but was also found with
viewers of first-generation camgirls where the number of web-page
hits did not clearly represent the degree of audience engagement
(Senft 2008). With first-generation camgirls, broadcasting still
images at fixed intervals minutes apart, these streams were not
meant to be viewed with the deep attention of a film in a cinema
or performance in a gallery. Instead, these refreshed, ongoing feeds
enabled viewers to easily dip in and out, opening and observing
(or not) while partaking in other activities. That is not to state that

hyper attention means lack of engagement with streams, but that the durational qualities of experiencing streams differs from other media. In addition, while the viewer has the option to move between tabs, the streamer carries on with the broadcast, as the aesthetics of duration become manifest in the exhaustion and transformation of the streamer's body, batteries, and data feeds. Thus, livestreaming functions as a distinctive form of the aesthetics of duration, both for the streamer and the viewer, enabling parallel yet interconnected experiences of time mediated through technical objects in a shared aesthetic encounter. This cross section of time can lead to physical exhaustion, as our bodies become attuned to technical objects that counter familiar actions, but can also open possibilities of how time is used to capture and alter attention. This latter point evokes what Yves Citton (2017) refers to as an ecology of attention, which focuses on how attention produces individuals rather than economizing attention as a scarce resource. While the capacity of livestreaming to enable social-justice movements to cultivate relations is no longer confined by the restrictions of geography, other significant, if overlooked, possibilities also emerge: the ability to engage with livestreaming to cultivate a new grassroots ecology of attention through the cross section of temporal scales.

When Death Goes Viral

WHILE LIVESTREAMING has been used as a means of building activist networks for social justice, in other instances streamed videos have become the impetus for action. On July 6, 2016, Diamond Reynolds began streaming on Facebook as Officer Jeronimo Yanez aimed his gun at her. He had just shot and killed her boyfriend Philando Castile during a routine traffic stop. Shortly thereafter, an archived version of the stream went viral across social media, sparking outcry and protests across the United States. The affective implications of this video, "merged with the momentum of the still fresh videos of the killing of Alton Sterling who had been shot roughly forty-four hours earlier in Baton Rouge, Louisiana" became the impetus for political action (Kumanyika 2017, 169). Within an hour of her stream, Reynold's video received thousands of views and shares, and within days this number reached millions. These online viewers are what Sam Gregory (2015) refers to as distant witnesses, who are "copresent" through the livestreamed video, both synchronously as it is broadcast and asynchronously as it is played back and shared over social media. Distant witnesses have the capacity to impact events. In the case of Reynold's stream, they instigated protests across the United States.

The video bears the stylistic qualities of being produced in the moment. The camera framing is close, too close, with visibly shaky movements that contrast with the steady tone of Reynolds's voice.

Only fragments of the unfolding events are evident (which I am intentionally not recounting here), but the emotional intensity and distress of the situation is clear. There is an incongruity with the final part of the video, which occurs once the phone is placed on the ground and the camera is still recording after Reynolds leaves the car, presenting a clear blue sky crossed with overhead electrical wires. At one point, the phone is forgotten, yet continues to stream. The camera streams for several more minutes, showing the unchanging frame of the blue sky, until someone picks up the phone and turns off the camera.

When this video went viral, I noticed how some of my white friends on social media shared it, highlighting the need to watch it in order to view these racist injustices. At times, people commented on how the video made them uncomfortable, but they made sure to watch it all the way through. There is an underlying presumption that witnessing such atrocities is necessary for white and non-Black viewers to acknowledge racism and how racist violence exists. Such statements give me pause regarding how these videos circulate online. Christina Sharpe describes how the repetition of imagery presenting "quotidian and extraordinary cruel and unusual violences enacted on Black people does not lead to a cessation of violence, nor does it, across or within communities, lead primarily to sympathy or something like empathy. Such repetitions often work to solidify and make continuous the colonial project of violence" (Sharpe 2016, 116).

Videos such as these evoke Susan Sontag's short book, *Regarding the Pain of Others*, in which she considers photographic imagery and suffering. She wrote this book in 2003, at a time when blogging and Internet self-publishing were becoming more popular, though just prior to the advent of major social media platforms that facilitated the mass uploading and sharing of user-generated content. At that stage, videos and photographs in the media were no longer confined solely to the authority of journalists—a process that was further advanced through the dissemination of digital cameras in smartphones, perhaps the most ubiquitous piece of digital hardware in the current moment. Sontag discusses the impact of war photography, pointing out the multiplicity of responses that such images may evoke: "Photographs of an atrocity may give rise to opposing responses. A call for peace. A cry for revenge. Or simply the bemused awareness, continually restocked by photographic information, that terrible things happen" (Sontag 2003, 13). While such images may play a significant role in raising awareness and lead to social responses, lens-based depictions of suffering do not result in clear uptake that stops the represented violence.

Sontag notes how photography and photojournalism did not bring the end of warfare during the nineteenth and twentieth centuries, as some had hoped, despite the increased authority that lens-based media carries. This authority connects to the camera's capacity to merge objectivity with a subjective point of view, functioning as a "record of the real—incontrovertible, as no verbal account, however impartial, could be—since a machine was doing the recording. And they bore witness to the real—since a person had been there to take them" (Sontag 2003, 26). Today's livestreaming compounds these qualities of authenticity, where "pictures of hellish events seem even more authentic when they don't have the look that comes from being 'properly' lighted and composed, because the photographer [or streamer] either is an amateur or—just as serviceable—has adopted one of several familiar anti-art styles" (Sontag 2003, 26–27), through the shortening of time between event and its presentation. As such, these images are considered less manipulative than staged presentations of suffering, as through fictional films, where considerations of style are used explicitly to influence audience reactions. The role of lens-based media is poignant and its aesthetic impact exceeds the frame of the image. However, it cannot be forgotten that Reynolds's video presents a murder, and her act of livestreaming most likely prevented another one.

To consider this video in terms of a relational aesthetic encounter also raises ethical questions around sharing such content online. These scenes are experienced as shared sensory phenomena. Drawing from Rancière (2014), politics revolves around what can

be seen and what can be said, with aesthetics enabling such processes of making sensible. The presentation of information, for
Simondon, involves operations of taking on form, which is anal-
ogous to Rancière's relationship of the aesthetic and the political:
information forms as it informs. In other words, Reynolds's stream
and subsequent shared video makes visible police racist violence
and murder, but also is an instance of how those targeted by this
violence produce videos that extend the scope of witnessing these
experiences. These videos are transformative not just because of
the content, but *who* produces them and *whose* voices can be heard.

There is a paradox to this visibility, however, that Rancière does
not consider, and has implications for marginalized and minoritized groups and individuals. In her book, *Dark Matters: On the
Surveillance of Blackness*, Simone Browne traces a genealogy of
surveilling Black bodies to the transatlantic slave trade, where the
visibility of Black individuals is used as a means of instigating racist
oppression: "Surveillance is nothing new to black folks. It is the
fact of antiblackness" (Browne 2015, 10). To make visible means
to make trackable and controllable, which predates the technological infrastructures and algorithmic mediation of social media.
In addition, these broadcasts perpetuate a "terrible spectacle" of
violence, which Sadiya Hartman relates to slavery in the United
States, where the origin of enslaved subjects was tied to violence as a
means of demonstrating the "brutal power and authority of another"
(Hartman 1997, 3). The "terrible spectacle" of violence against the
enslaved persists in videos and images of violence against Black
individuals online, continuing to define subjectivity through brutal
violence and death. When discussing such depictions of violence
against the enslaved, Hartman asks if we are witnesses to the truth
of such trauma, or "are we voyeurs fascinated with and repelled by
exhibitions of terror and suffering?" (Hartman 1997, 3). The legacy
of slavery remains as the "afterlife of slavery":

> If slavery persists as an issue in the political life of black America, it
> is not because of an antiquarian obsession with bygone days or the
> burden of a too-long memory, but because black lives are still im-

periled and devalued by a racial calculus and a political arithmetic that were entrenched centuries ago. This is the afterlife of slavery—skewed life chances, limited access to health and education, premature death, incarceration, and impoverishment (Hartman 2007, 6).

Here, I want to return to the title of Sontag's book, regarding the pain of *others*. Sontag connects war photography to a longer iconography of suffering, arguing that "it seems that the appetite for pictures showing bodies in pain is as keen, almost, as the desire for ones that show bodies naked" (Sontag 2003, 41). Witnessing an image of suffering created with a camera implies that whoever is viewing this image is at a different time and place than when the images were documented, though with livestreaming the gap in time has become much narrower, to less than a minute. Sontag considers who has the right to witness such pain, noting that: "Perhaps the only people with the right to look at images of suffering of this extreme order are those who can alleviate it [. . .] or those who could learn from it. The rest of us are voyeurs, whether or not we mean to be" (Sontag 2003, 42). When viewing Diamond Reynolds's video, I am witnessing the trauma of an other as it unfolds. The other in this instance is not just because it is violence occurring to someone different from I, but also as a white person living in a European country, I am not subjected to the systemic racism that influences police brutality in the United States. Viewing the archived stream, I am not just witnessing someone else's trauma, but become a spectator to the racist violence Black people experience from Reynolds's perspective. I engage in shared emotional distress by watching this video (Sutherland 2017), but I cannot limit the ethical implications of this video to my emotional state. Instead I ask: Do I have a right to view this trauma? Can I alleviate it? Can I learn from it? Or am I a voyeur? In addition to being emotionally impacted by this video, am I partaking in the necessary actions to instigate change? What would it mean for me to share and circulate this video on social media? What are the consequences of sharing this video and its capacity to re-traumatize? And to be discussed further below, who profits from me sharing this viral video? Here is what Hartman refers to as the "uncertain line between witness and spectator" and the "precariousness of empathy" in responding to such depictions of violence, especially when depictions of such trauma define Black subjectivity (Hartman 1997, 4).

The Commodification of Trauma

The gestures of sharing videos of racist violence on social media by white individuals may assuage guilt, though even the most well-meaning allies risk perpetuating violence against Black bodies and the spectacle of anti-Black violence in order to satisfy white affect. In addition, Sofiya Noble (2018) argues that the structure of social media platforms as private corporate enterprises means that profit is being made through the sharing of collective trauma. Social media sites are part of what Jean Burgess refers to as the platform paradigm, which means "not only that platforms like YouTube and Facebook have a lot of power within the information sector and creative content industries but also that their *logic*—their ways of operating and their systems of value—are more deeply reshaping our society and culture" (Burgess 2021, 22). When livestreams are presented on social media platforms, they function as part of this datafied ecosystem and exist beyond the intentions and influence of the creators, enabling the "extraction and collection of digital traces of cultural practices and social interactions so that they can be sorted, aggregated, analyzed, and deployed for strategic purposes" (Burgess 2021, 22–23). The technical objects of livestreaming, therefore, not only include the hardware involved in the creation and viewing of broadcasts, but the platforms that store and circulate them. The role of social media platforms in the framing and datafication of these streams, including the risk of perpetuating trauma through the viral circulation of media, warrants further attention.

If, as Susan Sontag states, "photographs objectify: they turn an event or a person into something that can be possessed" (Sontag 2003, 81), then images and videos, including the archive of Reynold's stream, that are posted on social media take this to a new extreme as digital objects. Yuk Hui defines digital objects as "basically data, sharable and controllable; they can be made visible or invisible through the configuration of the system" (Hui 2016, 1). That is, digital objects are not just comprised of content and form, such as video, sound, graphics, or text, but also their existence within digital infrastructures. Noble (2018) challenges the presumed benefits of sharing these traumatic videos and images online, arguing that such benefits tend to serve white audience members and corporate social media stakeholders. While Reynolds's livestream brought awareness to the disproportionate impact of police brutality on Black individuals in the United States to white audiences without direct experience of this violence, the circulation of the video did not serve as evidence against Castile's killers (Alexander and Alexander 2021). Tonia Sutherland argues that through social media "death and trauma are continuously re-inscribed, visually and, perhaps, eternally," reinforcing the systems of racism and white supremacy that cause such deaths (Sutherland 2017, 34). Like a gif that repeats the same action over and over, the viral circulation of these images repeat trauma as an infinite loop—violence against Black bodies becomes social media spectacle without recourse for justice.

Whether livestreams are used to build activist networks and support protest on the ground or become the impetus for such actions, the techno-aesthetics of livestreams shot and shared on social media networks are entangled in milieux that are material and social, political and ethical. These streams extend the realm of political possibility through the aesthetic object of moving image, as encounters with these objects enable ways of redefining engagement. At the same time, there is risk of reinforcing white, supremacist, capitalist oppression. Ruha Benjamin observes how white supremacy is encoded in digital technologies through the "new Jim Code," or "the employment of new technologies that reflect and reproduce existing inequities but that are promoted and perceived as more objective or progressive than the discriminatory systems of a previous era" (Benjamin 2019, 3). Instead of technology bypassing human biases, ideologies and values, including white supremacy, are encoded into technologies, with the ability to entrench and perpetuate them at speeds and capacities that exceed previous forms of social relations. While livestreaming is a vital aspect of social movements today, the form is implicated in commercial and institutional structures that risk perpetuating the injustices that people and groups may be trying to counter, as the techno-aesthetics of these streams are influenced by these structures.

Performative Allyship

Even in instances where outrage leads to action, what is becoming more often the case is the *appearance* of action. The neologism performative allyship, or "the practice of announcing or demonstrating allyship for an audience" (Jackson, Bailey, and Welles 2020, 168), has come to describe online activism lacking offline counterparts. Mia Mckenzie (2015) argues that performative allyship, or what she refers to as "ally theatre," provides a glimpse into the shortcomings of white allyship more generally speaking, where the need to be seen performing allyship publicly takes precedence over real solidarity. While the phrase has been in circulation for some time, the response to racist police brutality and murder during the Covid-19 pandemic has brought criticisms of such online gestures into sharp focus. The issue that performative allyship raises is not that digital technologies and their entangled performances are inadequate platforms and tools for activism. Instead, performative allyship exemplifies when social justice becomes personal performances of impression management online. Here, aesthetics is reduced to the stylistic impressions of an individual when performing the role of allyship rather than the multifaceted encounter that livestreaming provokes. That is, acts of allyship are reduced to being *seen* as an ally. An example of this includes the sharing of Reynolds's archived stream coupled with statements by white viewers of the need to witness this video that are directed toward other white viewers. Performative allyship satisfies the need to be seen as supporting social movements—allyship with an audience.

Sara Ahmed's work pertaining to diversity in educational institutions provides a useful way of rethinking J. L. Austin's performative in conjunction with performative allyship. Austin defines a performative utterance as when a person "is *doing* something rather than merely saying something" (emphasis in original, Austin 1979, 235). His treatment of words as the means of performing actions treats language as a constitutive gesture as opposed to just being relegated to a realm of description or reflection. In *On Being Included: Racism and Diversity in Institutional Life* (2012), Ahmed considered institutional approaches to diversity through Austin's definition of the performative. In particular, Ahmed describes how an institutional policy pertaining to diversity and statements about diversity, such as "we are diverse," come to take the place of action to make the necessary changes to implement diversity. Such statements may be considered as paying lip service to diversity, much like performative allyship, where the creating and sharing of digital objects on social media take the place of the actual deliverables of social justice. However, while Austin does not consider statements of lip service as pertaining to the performative, as they do not *do* what is stated, Ahmed argues that these statements change the conventions of speaking about diversity, though not always in ways to accommodate appropriate actions. In a similar manner, acts of performative allyship change ways of speaking about social justice online, altering the conventions of social media. However, there is simultaneously a reinforcing of the norms of white supremacy as personal reputation takes precedence over the necessary alterations of habits required for change to occur.

The Aesthetics and Ethics of Allyship

Like the educational institution, the individual on social media is concerned about the presentation of self, which is a performance of impression management. Emphasis comes to be placed on being seen as performing, which correlates with a general rise in performance culture. Performance culture involves "increasing

self-consciousness about how to perform in [audit] systems, by
generating the right kinds of procedures, methods, and materials,
where rightness is determined as the fulfillment of the require-
ments of a system" (Ahmed 2012, 84–85). What originated in the
financial sector, Ahmed observes, has transitioned to public institutions with an increased reliance on audit systems, including
universities, but is now centered on individuals through emphasis
on self-improvement. It also means to be seen as performing, where
to "do well" means "generating *the right kinds of appearance*" (emphasis in original, Ahmed 2012, 85). Ahmed warns that this sort of
performance culture can in fact conceal inequalities, such as when
emphasis is placed on being *perceived* as anti-racist in instances
of performative allyship. At the same time, Ahmed acknowledges
the significance of going through the actions affiliated with performance culture: "If equality can be a way of 'going through the
motions,' these motions give the institution a direction; the motions
themselves direct attention" (Ahmed 2012, 111). Trouble arises when
this shift in attention is perceived as an end in itself.

What role does aesthetics play in this? As noted previously, performative allyship is a type of impression management, where the
user develops allyship as a brand and greater attention is paid to
the virtual impression of allyship rather than engaging in actions
that lead to accountable change. Here, the design of social media
platforms influences how content is presented and shared, impact-
ing the style of such content, which includes being shown as part
of a never-ending feed of content. Topics in the social media feed
switch as quickly as a person scrolls through them, facilitating hyper
attention. Emphasis is placed on capturing attention, which is an
aspect of the aesthetic encounter that focuses on visual and aural
stimuli and sensations. Someone posting the need to watch a video
is one way to capture attention in this context. Once re-shared, a
livestream becomes recontextualized, not just as a means of extending the audience of virtual witnesses to murder and a perpetuation of the spectacle of death as defining Black subjectivity, but
also enabling the person sharing to identify as an ally. This change

in context within the technological milieu shifts the aesthetic encounter from the video itself to the impression management of the
person sharing it.

Not all acts of social justice online are to be treated as equal.
This leads to the question: Is a more authentic or ethical means of
sharing content online possible, and if so, what would it look like?
Considering the current design of technological infrastructures
that make livestreaming possible and the values encoded into these
technologies, which facilitate allyship as brand management, a radical shift in how they are used is needed. As aesthetic *encounters*,
livestreams cannot be simply reduced to fixed interpretations, even
though these are presented on social media and are archived as
digital objects. With each experience of engagement, new possibilities for relation occur. That is, aesthetic encounters entail relational complexities and possibilities for future becomings that
cannot be simply reduced to calculation, like the number of views
or comments, entangled with the ethical and political relations of
transindividuation vital for social justice. Livestreaming's aesthetics of duration, as discussed previously, could provide one means
of working against the grain of current social media platforms.
Here duration is not just in terms of the style of streams, but also
to consider social justice itself a kind of durational performance of
which livestreams function as one part of a broader milieu of people,
technical objects, geographies, and social systems. Emphasis is not
just on the stream itself, but the relational implications and interactions that include the virtual realm along with what happens offline.

Patternmaking: Techno-Aesthetics of Mundane Intimacy

THE SEVERE ACUTE RESPIRATORY SYNDROME CORONAVIRUS 2 (SARS-CoV-2), which causes Covid-19, is a living, agential being: a "positive-sense single-stranded RNA virus with epithelial cell and respiratory system proclivity" (Machhi et al. 2020). It spreads rapidly from human to human, carried in droplets passed through coughing, sneezing, hand contact with eyes or mouth, and contaminated surfaces. From the lungs, it spreads through blood to other organs, including the kidneys, liver, muscles, nervous system, and spleen. Since the initial outbreak, vaccines have been developed and there are various therapeutic care options, but the virus also evolves as it spreads, producing variants. As a living, agential being, the virus is not a fixed entity, but undergoes processes of transduction and individuation. The Covid-19 pandemic revealed human interdependencies and shared vulnerabilities, making such relational connections undeniable. These interdependencies and vulnerabilities do not just emerge in regard to biological entities. Ruha Benjamin refers to Covid-19 as a "social disease" that also reveals the inadequacies of shared systems of world-making where "ableism, racism, sexism, classism, and colonialism work to eliminate unwanted people" (Benjamin 2022, 10).

What does this have to do with the primary focus of this book: livestreaming? This short book began during the Covid-19 pandemic

as part of an inquiry into engagement with livestreaming as a significant means of synchronous connection for many. It shifted from
being, prior to the pandemic, a tool used when necessary, though
begrudgingly, to the norm of interaction. What these uses of livestreaming revealed, however, was an undeniability of interdependencies with technical systems and shared vulnerabilities that have
already existed. The relations experienced through livestreaming
are different than those experienced otherwise, which can be said
of the phenomenology of relating through and with technical objects generally. This difference of experience evoked a curiosity in
me, not just in how it impacted us in the moments of engagement,
but how this influenced our becoming together. Therefore, I end
this book with the discussion of a performance artist, Ayana Evans,
who began engaging with livestreaming over Instagram during the
first Covid-19 lockdown of 2020. Evans's performance practice is
rooted in live, in-person engagement with her audience—she regularly instructs audience members to carry her or hold her and wel-
comes participation in shared actions such as doing jumping jacks
or push-ups together. However, when public health restrictions
prevented in-person performances from taking place, she engaged
with livestreaming in order to continue producing art. Different
from producing performances to camera, which is its own genre of
artmaking, livestreaming enabled the dynamic interaction with her
audience that performance art affords. Through this process, Evans
does not just engage with technical objects, but through her techno-
aesthetics of mundane intimacy, she engages with an ethics of care,
functioning as what Benjamin (2022) refers to as a patternmaker:
one who creates new patterns of being and becoming together.

Evans starts her first streamed performance of her five-week
"Quarantine Series," *New York Living* (April 2020), wearing her
signature yellow zebra-striped catsuit and full makeup.[1] She holds

1. Since 2012, Evans has been performing the "Operation Catsuit"
series, in which she dons a neon yellow Zebra body stocking. The catsuit
has become an iconic garment of her performances, which functions as "her

the smartphone close to her face, which like other streams discussed thus far, makes the camera *too* close. The smartphone is in selfie mode, which utilizes the front-facing camera to enable the stream-er to view themselves on the screen while shooting. She quickly breaks down illusions of a hermetically sealed performance space, speaking to her audience and asking if enough people are present for her to begin. She then gives a brief tour of her studio apartment, moving the smartphone camera rapidly around the room. It is im-possible to get a full sense of the apartment's size and layout from the framing on the screen. Instead, this sequence emphasizes the confinement of the space through the inability to stand back. Evans grabs her window blinds, stating that she is redecorating and that these actions are part of the performance. She is conscientious of the virtual audience's presence and need for staging when creating a performance, but she does not hide the labor that goes into setting up her space as she prepares for her actions in and out of the camera frame as part of the stream. She engages in mundane chatter that is intimate and personal, drawing connections with the dispersed virtual audience. Evans names specific individuals who text her as she performs, highlighting the indiscernibility of life and art. After putting on a pair of black heels, Evans picks up the window blinds and stands on a chair, looking down at the camera as the height of her body fills the frame. She waves the blinds like a flag, then begins to cut them. The blinds come apart in her hands, hitting objects as she waves them back and forth with her gestures becoming increas-ingly frantic. Her interactions with the blinds draw attention to the confinement of the space and camera frame, as the cacophonous sound blends with music playing in the background. At one point, she directly addresses her audience and encourages them to post emojis. She speaks of her recent challenges of being sick (Evans had contracted Covid-19 during March 2020, when much about

---

art scene uniform. [. . .] It helps make her a more recognizable figure in the performance art scene in New York City, and more, donning it acts as a cue that she is going to work" (Rodney 2020).

the virus was still unknown) and how the university that employed her at the time did not pay enough to cover her medical insurance, alluding to the challenges that precarious academic staff face in the United States. This combination of seemingly unrelated performance gestures with social critique adds affective weight to the breaking down of the blinds, an object that becomes increasingly unwieldy the more she tries to deconstruct it. She poses with the blinds, wearing them as a sculptural garment, then brings her hand close to the camera and shows a cut she received from the action, which she cleans with a banana peel. The performance ends when Evans turns off the camera.

Evans does not just perform to the camera, but *with* livestreaming technologies. The camera is not a means of documentation, but the technical objects and systems of the smartphone and social media open a virtual site of performance and mediate the relations that take place within this shared techno-geographic milieu. Through this process, she cultivates aesthetic encounters that offer different means of engaging with these technologies. Evans's streams can be found on social media platforms, where she engages with technological affordances to facilitate interactions with her virtual audience. In certain ways, her works are evocative of social media content creators, particularly her engagement with an aesthetics of mundane intimacy. These aesthetics of mundane intimacy are not just a stylistic decision based on the performer's choices, as techno-aesthetics are connected to the technical objects of livestreaming. Through this process, Evans functions as a patternmaker. Not only does she alter the patterns of content online through her aesthetic encounters, as her work stands apart from other social media content, but she also introduces new patterns of social relations that are political and ethical, even when the content is not explicit as such.

Instagram, which Evans used to stream her Quarantine Series, has affordances that simplify the process both for producing and watching livestreams. In order to go live on Instagram, someone only needs to click the option on a screen and the stream begins.

The interface displays the stream in portrait format, which is also the way it is presented. Even though it is possible to stream from either the smartphone's back- or front-facing camera, the portrait mode frames and displays the human face most effectively. That does not mean that all streamers will engage with the technology in this manner, but the formal and material qualities of the technical objects invite this type of interaction. Instagram streams are also designed to be viewed on a smartphone device. Followers receive notification that a stream has begun, unlike Zoom which requires invitations and specific links. The small screen of the smartphone is held in the palm of the hand, designed to be engaged with in less than arm's length. The smartphone has a touchscreen as an interface, which is tapped and stroked by the user whose fingers caress the glass. If there is already a distinctive kind of intimacy to Internet broadcasts through the closeness of the camera, the smartphone invites yet other kinds of mundane intimacy through its affordances.

This intimacy invites different types of audience engagement from the gallery context. During livestreams, and particularly on Instagram, audience members participated through their shared virtual presence, making comments and observations that reveal inner monologues or chattering among each other about the actions, which would be considered rude or inappropriate in a gallery context but is commonplace within social media. Evans observes how Instagram also enabled her to extend her audience geographically and include people from different spheres of her life, as family members from across the country were able to now witness her perform live. She notes how those who would tune in regularly developed a bond over time, coming to know each other within this virtual space.[2] As a result, there is a means of participating in performance for both artist and audience that differs from the in-person context.

2. Unpublished interview of Ayana Evans with author over Zoom, August 18, 2022.

"Masks, Gloves, Soap, Scrubs"

In her final performance of the Quarantine Series, Evans both directly engages with social media content while standing apart from it. Like her previous performances of the series, the image is framed in portrait style and is in selfie mode. The phone moves as she handles it and interacts with a material off-camera—the crinkles and stretching noise of tape. Evans tapes her smartphone to the ceiling, commenting on how it serves a similar function as a drone, providing a bird's-eye view of her bed. For the first part of the performance, music begins to play, with lyrics reflecting the new material reality of Covid-19: "masks, gloves, soap, scrubs, masks, gloves, soap, scrubs." The song is by drag queen Todrick Hall. Evans, wearing her yellow zebra stripe catsuit, red heels, and a feather boa, dances and poses with masks and blue gloves while lying down in bed. She then pretends to spray a cleaner around her space, dancing in relation to the music. Comparing Evan's livestreamed performances to Todrick Hall's music video highlights significant aesthetic differences between these two forms of online media.

Hall's music video opens with them standing in a bedroom, the shot framed in portrait format. This video does not fill the frame of the screen, but instead there is black space later filled with the videos of other people dancing. The video is well edited to the pace of the music, comprised of footage shot on smartphones later collaged. Video tiles shift and change in rhythm to the music, with colors at times pulsating in the background. Some dancers wear color-coordinated costumes and present their moves with a choreographed flourish. Other dancers include people in very casual clothing, making it evident that they have not left the house for some time, while others are drag queens in full dress. In contrast to the choreographed moves of the first part of the video, these latter dancers present gestures that relate to the lyrics—spray for me spray for me, fold clothes for me clothes for me, get away from me away from me away—presenting their actions in comedic and exaggerated ways. The video, song, and various performers are playful and humorous, which was common for many videos circulating in social media at this time, coping with and providing relief for the extreme, ongoing stress of the pandemic. Hall's video is edited to emphasize its pithy humor, encapsulating a condensed performance that is entertaining, designed to appeal to large audiences, and to go viral, which this particular video did.

In contrast, Evans's streams do not involve such features of post-production, as she slips between performed actions through unedited improvisation of the livestream. Evan's differentiating qualities become even more explicit in the second part of the stream, as she transitions from the more recognizable gestures of Hall's music video to her own idiosyncratic actions which involve her interacting with food items, including cinnamon swirl toast and a banana. Evans eats the food, throws it to the ceiling, stuffs it into her mouth, and rubs it onto her face. At certain points, she holds her hand close to the camera, squishing the banana, though the shot is out of focus, as she is too close for the smartphone camera to properly adjust. The camera and screen invite a closeness with the performer, where she connects with multiple individuals simultaneously with the same gesture. Evans takes advantage of the distinctiveness of digital intimacy.

Part of her process of streaming performances involved experimentation with what worked well on camera but also live. This process involved inevitable moments of failure, but also enabled Evans to explore ways of engaging with technical objects and her audience. For instance, through the experiences of livestreaming regularly, Evans realized that contrasting the framing of her actions between close-up and far away in the frame of the shot did not work well over the smartphone camera, with audience members losing interest as Evans stepped back. Other shots, such as extreme close-ups of the eye and holding a pair of scissors close to the face conveyed a sense of risk that gave rise to audience responses, despite the fact that this gesture posed no harm to her.[3]

---

3. Unpublished interview of Ayana Evans with author over Zoom, August 18, 2022.

Unlike the cam girls, who hacked and modified technical objects to repurpose them for webcasting, the streaming technologies of today are designed for broadcasting online, presenting a more accessible yet technically closed system. However, as noted in the introduction, this shared techno-geographics milieu is not just material, but also the immaterial relations that connect to broader social and cultural systems.

Aesthetics of Mundane Intimacy as Transformative

Evans's streamed performances present a capacity to transform the everyday, as artist and philosopher Adrian Piper does in her interventionist *Catalysis* series (1970–1972). In this series, Piper presented socially offensive, understated interventions, including soaking her clothes in raw eggs, vinegar, milk, and cod liver oil for a week, and then wearing these garments on the New York City Subway during rush hour (*Catalysis I*); shopping for gloves and sunglasses at Macy's while wearing a shirt coated in white paint with a cardboard sign that states "Wet Paint" (*Catalysis III*); dressing in conservative business attire and riding public transit with a towel stuffed in her mouth and sticking out (*Catalysis IV*); and walking around the Metropolitan Museum of Art wearing a tight skirt and heels while popping bubblegum so that it coats her face while carrying a handbag full of ketchup (*Catalysis VII*). In these performances, which were presented outside the gallery context and without indication that these actions were art, Piper turns nonart objects and scenarios into aesthetic encounters. Art here is not a reflection of society or representation of it, but an intervention into social relations, which as aesthetic encounters enables different means of perceiving and understanding these relations while modifying through action. Even though these performances took place in public spaces where strangers tend to maintain distance through social convention, Piper's interventions infiltrate these boundaries through her sensory offenses, inviting unexpected intimacy.

Like Piper, Evans's performance practice involves highlighting social interactions through aesthetic interventions, twisting these interactions (which for the "Quarantined Series" include virtual social interactions) revealing shared systems. The gestures and actions may be rooted in mundane intimacy, but also constitute what art theorist and critic Jack Burnham terms systems aesthetics. Burnham (1968) first coined the phrase during the late 1960s in response to the increased emphasis on systems thinking in the mid-twentieth century, including cybernetics. Systems aesthetics was a means by which artists adopt the logic of systems thinking and "even directly infiltrate existing systems to transform them from within" (Gosse and Stott 2021, 5).

These interventions can function as what Ruha Benjamin describes as patternmaking: "if inequity and injustice are woven into the very fabric of society, then each twist, coil, and code offers a chance for us to weave new patterns, practices, and politics . . . new blueprints. The vastness of the problems we face will be their undoing when we accept that we are patternmakers" (Benjamin 2022, 283). Such practices include grand gestures, but also, and perhaps even more importantly for Benjamin, the subtle everyday interactions that comprise daily relations on a micro level. Throughout her performance oeuvre, Evans's repurposing of mundane objects and actions create atypical scenarios for social interaction that reveal prejudices and biases with focus on the impact of systemic racism on Black women and femmes (shakur 2018; Rodney 2020). For instance, she makes the labor of Black women visible through prolonged durational periods of repetitive physical exercise in a yellow zebra catsuit and heels, as in the ten-hour performance *Throwing Hexes* (2017), or presenting such exercises in atypical scenarios, as in her series *Stopping Traffic* (2016, 2020), where she performs chair dips in the middle of busy streets wearing an evening gown. Like Piper's *Catalysis* series, Evans's interventions test the limits of conventions and challenge the constructions of these conventions. A continuation of her non-virtual actions, Evans's livestreamed performances exist as part of the new biological, geographic, social, and technological milieu of

Covid-19, where engagement with the techno-aesthetics of mundane intimacy enable system interventions.

Evans describes on her website that when she began livestreaming performance, she did not just try to recreate her habitual participatory performances for video, but approached it as a problem that arose from her immediate circumstances (Evans n.d.). As noted in chapter one, Simondon refers to transduction as individuation in process, which occurs within a physical domain. He states: "transduction does not go elsewhere to seek a principle to resolve the problem of a domain: it extracts the resolving structure from the very tensions of this domain" (Simondon 2020, 15). To consider Evans's livestreamed performances in this way, her practice engages with the physical domain—including her geographic locality, the Covid-19 virus, her body, and technical objects—as well as the social structures of racism and misogynoir in the United States, in order to face the problem that emerged for many people at this time: how to interact with people when needing to stay physically distant from others? There are immediate ethical implications here, as livestreaming became a means to restrict the spread of illness, but this is only a fraction of the possibilities of ethical relations that livestreaming introduces. Treating livestreaming as a performed aesthetic encounter that is relational and technological not only considers who we are, but who we have the potential to become, thereby also making it a speculative ethical encounter to imagine what is possible.

What it means to engage with each other is modified through relations with technical objects. In her response to pandemic restrictions, Kathleen Lynch laments how lack of physical engagement and touch "eliminated a key means by which we cocreate each other in intimate nurturing relations" (Lynch 2022, 216). Lynch argues that such relations are de-physical, with digital technologies unable to effectively fulfill the deficit, despite the ongoing efforts to do so. While I acknowledge the significance of these points, especially when technologies could be used to take on caring responsibilities as a replacement for humans due to advancements in machine learning, sensor technologies, and robotics, I challenge Lynch's assertion that such relations are de-physical. Rather than being de-physical, such relations involve a different kind of physicality and intimate relationality, as Evans's practice makes evident. Perhaps the issue here is not the inability of technologies to fill a deficit of touch, but the desire for these technologies to do so in a similar way that occurs with in-person physical touch. Here the consideration of livestreaming as a distinctive aesthetic encounter can enable ways of imagining other ways of relating with and through technology, ones that engage with and acknowledge particular material existences, agencies, and individuations of such objects and systems for a differentiating ethics of digital touch.

Exceeding Quantification

As a performance artist, Evans does not present her actions with the intention of simply entertaining her audience, capturing their attention to go viral. Generally, when content creators present such gestures, videos are edited in order to highlight impact and presented in a manner that minimizes discomfort to engage with the widest audience possible, as is evident with Hall's music video. As livestreams, Evans's videos are not edited, and like performance art that takes place in a gallery, the unfolding of the actions over time evoke a range of emotional responses—possibly transitioning from confusion and discomfort to pleasure and anticipation with potential moments of boredom—as the audience comes to terms with what is being witnessed, experiencing it as an aesthetic encounter. Performance art enables Evans to produce encounters that are thick in complexity through her idiosyncratic actions, engaging with materials and a gestural language that she has developed through her practice as an artist. Noel Fitzpatrick argues that such aesthetic experiences exceed quantification as "there are modes of mediation in the world which lie outside measurability and calculation" (Fitzpatrick 2021, 124). Within this context, technologies are engaged with differently in order to "enable reflection, deliberation,

conflict and reason" (Fitzpatrick 2021, 124). Evans is a patternmaker, which include the visual patterns like the yellow zebra stripe of
her catsuit and other stylistic considerations in the staging of her
performances, but also the repurposing of everyday objects and
playful gestural actions as exploration, her experimentations with
livestreaming technologies, and her ways of connecting to others
and with others, all constituting processes of transindividuation.
Meaning, therefore, cannot be simply extracted from her work, but
instead requires a viewer to sit with and engage with it in ambivalent
and ambiguous ways that cannot be easily quantified. In addition,
there is a gap between the range of aesthetic sensations a viewer
may experience and what can be captured through social media
metrics, with the latter only enabling viewers to input comments
or hit the like button. This gap is significant as it maintains that
there is *something* to this encounter that exceeds the quantifying
metrics of these systems. Evans engages with the affordances of
livestreaming technologies on social media, though treating them as
a performance art scenario, where the differences that performance
art introduce invites an ethical encounter that takes advantage of
technological capacities while transforming ensembles of relations
through engagement with technical objects.

Conclusion: (Not) Becoming Machine

THE FORCED DIGITALITY of the Covid-19 pandemic period made video livestreaming, which had been a more peripheral means of synchronous contact prior to this pandemic, the predominant means of interaction with others. That is, even though digital technologies already had become ubiquitous for many, this engagement changed in 2020 as we became even more dependent on these networks of communication. Simondon emphasizes how technical objects function as mediators. It is essential to treat technologies with the same scholarly and critical scrutiny and expertise that we use in sociology and psychology in coming to understand human interactions. However, many times digital technologies like those that comprise livestreaming are taken for granted, considered merely as a means to an end, as opposed to grasping just how these tools shape relations, resulting in alienation from technologies. Simondon warns that such alienation is dangerous:

> the most powerful cause of alienation in the contemporary world resides in this misunderstanding of the machine, which is not an alienation caused by the machine, but by the non-knowledge of its nature and its essence, by way of its absence from the world of significations, and its omission from the table of values and concepts that make up culture (Simondon 2016, 16).

This is where aesthetics comes in, in particular Simondon's techno-aesthetics, where aesthetics is grounded in the engagement with technical objects. The aesthetic encounter is the means by which the sensations of world phenomena are experienced, which are inherently relational and therefore ethical.

I describe three techno-aesthetic modes in relation to livestreaming: glitch and noise, duration, and mundane intimacy. These three modes influence the encounters that livestreaming provokes, which are dynamic engagements of relations and transformative processes of becoming through a shared milieu. Moreover, techno-aesthetics are also techno-ethics in providing ways of countering alienation from streaming technologies, as the features of technological mediation are accounted for when considering aesthetic encounters: aesthetics are directly related to how technologies are *engaged with* and how they *act upon* the world, thereby also making such encounters ethical. The aesthetic experience is not simply restricted to the formal or stylistic qualities of a work; *how* technologies *function* is integral to this encounter. The glitch aesthetics of the camgirls, which resulted from breakdown of technical systems, are formal instances of these technologies in action, constituting and mediating relations of global milieu, while supported and modified through maintenance as care. At the same time, these broadcasts established digital aesthetics of duration and aesthetics of mundane intimacy, as camgirls streamed their lives uncensored, at times so up close and personal that the viewer is "too close to see" (White 2003).

As the technologies of livestreaming developed, becoming more accessible and ubiquitous, it took on a more prominent presence in different spheres of engagement, including social-justice activism. The techno-aesthetics of activist streaming is considered in terms of production, itself a durational performance that negotiates engagement with technologies through an unfolding milieu that relates virtual audiences to on-the-street activities. It also makes evident the different experiences of time that the virtual enables. While activist broadcasting shares some stylistic characteristics with slow media, particularly slow cinema and durational performance art through exceptionally long takes and lack of overarching

narrative structure, social media interfaces invite engagement from
viewers that cultivate hyper attention rather than the deep attention
that the more experimental forms of artistic production involve. I
raise these points to highlight how the aesthetics of this encounter,
which can be traced to first-generation camgirls, is a distinguishing
characteristic of how digital technologies mediate these encounters.
Understanding how these mechanisms function through these encounters can enhance activism's engagement with technology in the
ecology of attention, as grassroots efforts to counter the dominance
of hegemonic narratives and thereby modify the field of political
and ethical action.

I then shift from the role of livestreaming as social-justice action
to the livestreamed videos of police brutality and murder that may
instigate such activism. Diamond Reynolds's Facebook livestream
of Philando Castile's death raises significant questions regarding
the ethics surrounding the sharing of these streams on social media
platforms, both through the commodification of trauma and the
perpetuation of anti-Black violence as spectacle. These issues come
to the fore when the sharing of such content is involved in performative allyship, which itself functions as a performed aesthetic
encounter of online impression management. Aesthetic encounters,
therefore, are not simply experiences of form, but involve technological, political, and ethical relations.

Finally, the transformative capacities of aesthetic and ethical encounters are evident in the livestreamed performance work of Ayana
Evans, in particular the techno-aesthetics of mundane intimacy.
Streaming over Instagram, Evans's "Quarantine Series" diffracts
the aesthetics of social media content creation through her interventions into everyday technological relations. Her performances
make evident the new forms of intimacy that digital technologies
of livestreaming afford, while extending understandings of participation that reveal and expand her ecosystem of support and
community. Understanding livestreaming in this way highlights
this ongoing capacity to transform, individuate, transindividuate,
and become different. Even as people are shifting away from en-

gaging with livestreaming technologies, returning to more face-to-face engagements in the current moment, the aesthetic encounter of livestreaming challenges the alienation of digital technologies, cracking seamless interface design by revealing, acknowledging, and modifying technological engagement, encompassing a relational ethics of care.

Through this analysis of livestreaming as aesthetic and ethical encounter, I cannot help but think about the dependence on livestreaming video in many facets of work and social life after the start of the pandemic when it was treated as a panacea at a time when physical contact was limited. The transition to video calls to replace the in-person engagement of classrooms, meetings, conferences, seminars, and other formal gatherings was quick once public health restrictions were put into place. Even though this technology facilitates conversations with the ability to look at a person's face (if the camera is turned on), prolonged engagement with video calls reveal that these experiences are different. Livestreaming has also changed group communication through this different milieu. Simondon states:

> the living being resolves problems, not just by adapting, i.e. by modifying its relation to the milieu (like a machine is capable of doing), but by modifying itself, by inventing new internal structures, and by completely introducing itself into the axiomatic of vital problems. *The living individual is a system of individuation, an individuating system, and a system that is in the midst of undergoing the process of individuating* (emphasis in original, Simondon 2020, 7).

The problems that living beings experience cannot be resolved with a simple fix, a key stroke, or a change in mechanism. Human individuals are not static creatures; they are dynamic beings that are part of shifting ecologies. Even in a state of crisis, like the Covid-19 pandemic, when these always already present moments of flux are stark (there is no stability, only temporary metastability), there is an expectation to pivot and engage technologies to maintain a façade of business as usual. Though, humans are living beings and not machines—simple adaptation is not possible.

Acknowledgments

This book started in the midst of the Covid-19 pandemic, emerging from my relational engagements with many others who supported its transduction. Many thanks to my friends and colleagues at the Beverly Salon, Mobius Artists Group, Cosmotechnics Group, National University of Ireland Galway (especially Frances McCormack for starting and maintaining our daily online writing group), and Maynooth University. A special thank you to Judith Brodsky for including me in her 2021 College Art Association Panel, "Dismantling the Patriarchy, Bit by Bit," where I initially presented my research on the first generation camgirls and livestreaming. I have much gratitude for Kate Antosik-Parsons and Noel Fitzpatrick for reading drafts of this publication, as well as the two anonymous peer reviewers for their significant insights and suggestions. Finally, I thank my family, David, Sonja, and Laurel, for their ongoing support, love, and care.

Bibliography

Abbate, Janet. 1999. "Cold War and White Heat: The Origins and Meanings of Packet Switching." In The Social Shaping of Technology, ed. Donald MacKenzie and Judy Wajcman, 351–71. Buckingham, UK: Open University Press.

Ahmed, Sara. 2012. *On Being Included: Racism and Diversity in Institutional Life*. Durham, N.C.: Duke University Press.

Alexander, Leslie, and Michelle Alexander. 2021. "Fear." In *The 1619 Project: A New Origin Story*, ed. Nikole Hannah-Jones and New York Times Company, 97–121. New York: One World.

Auslander, Philip. 2008a. "Live and Technologically Mediated Performance." In *Cambridge Companion to Performance Studies*, 107–19. Cambridge: Cambridge University Press.

Auslander, Philip. 2008b. *Liveness: Performance in a Mediatized Culture*. London: Routledge.

Auslander, Philip. 2012. "Digital Liveness: A Historico-Philosophical Perspective." *PAJ: A Journal of Performance and Art* 102: 3–11.

Austin, J. L. 1979. "Performative Utterances." In *Philosophical Papers*, 233–52. Oxford: Oxford University Press.

Baran, Paul. 1964. "On Distributed Communications." Memorandum RM-3420-PR. Santa Monica, CA: RAND Corporation.

Benjamin, Ruha. 2019. *Race after Technology: Abolitionist Tools for the New Jim Code*. Newark, UK: Polity Press.

Benjamin, Ruha. 2022. *Viral Justice: How We Grow the World We Want*. Princeton, N.J.: Princeton University Press.

Bishop, Claire. 2012. *Artificial Hells: Participatory Art and the Politics of Spectatorship*. London: Verso.

brown, adrienne maree. 2017. *Emergent Strategy: Shaping Change, Changing Worlds*. Chico, Calif.: AK Press.

brown, adrienne maree. 2020. *We Will Not Cancel Us: And Other Dreams of Transformative Justice*. Chico, Calif.: AK Press.

Browne, Simone. 2015. *Dark Matters: On the Surveillance of Blackness.* Durham, N.C.: Duke University Press.

Burgess, Jean. 2021. "Platform Studies." In *Creator Culture: An Introduction to Global Social Media Entertainment,* ed. Stuart Cunningham and David Craig. New York: New York University Press.

Burgin, Victor. 2000. "Jenni's Room: Exhibitionism and Solitude." *Critical Inquiry* 27, no. 1 (Autumn): 77–89.

Burnham, Jack. 1968. "Systems Esthetics." *Artforum* 7, no. 1 (September): 30–35.

Chabot, Pascal. 2014. *The Philosophy of Simondon: Between Technology and Individuation.* Trans. Aliza Krefetz and Graeme Kirkpatrick. London: Bloomsbury.

Citton, Yves. 2017. *The Ecology of Attention.* Cambridge: Polity.

Combes, Muriel. 2013. *Gilbert Simondon and the Philosophy of the Transindividual.* Trans. Thomas LaMarre. Technologies of Lived Abstraction. Cambridge, Mass.: MIT Press.

Costanza-Chock, Sasha. 2012. "Mic Check! Media Cultures and the Occupy Movement." *Social Movement Studies* 11, no. 3–4 (August): 375–85. https://doi.org/10.1080/14742837.2012.710746.

De Boever, Arne, Alex Murray, Jon Roffe, and Ashley Woodward, eds. 2012. *Gilbert Simondon: Being and Technology.* Edinburgh: Edinburgh University Press.

Dean, Aria. 2016. "Closing the Loop." *The New Inquiry* (blog). March 1, 2016. https://thenewinquiry.com/closing-the-loop/.

Dean, Jodi. 2010. *Blog Theory: Feedback and Capture in the Circuits of Drive.* Cambridge: Polity.

Dixon, Steve. 2015. *Digital Performance: A History of New Media in Theater.* Cambridge, Mass.: MIT Press.

Evans, Ayana. n.d. "Quarantine Performance | Solo Actions." Ayana M. Evans. Accessed March 8, 2022. https://www.ayanaevans.com/3rd-gallery?pgid=iy6t336z-35f60925-1b1f-4db3-bed5-64bf155e5724.

Fitzpatrick, Noel. 2021. "The Neganthropocene: Introduction." In *Aesthetics, Digital Studies, and Bernard Stiegler,* edited by Noel Fitzpatrick, Néill O'Dwyer, and Mick O'Hara, 123–25. London: Bloomsbury.

Flanagan, Matthew. 2008. "Towards an Aesthetic of Slow in Contemporary Cinema." *16:9* 6, no. 29 (November). http://www.16-9.dk/2008-11/side11_inenglish.htm.

Gaskins, Nettrice. 2019. "Techno-Vernacular Creativity and Innovation across the African Diaspora and Global South." In *Captivating Technology: Race, Carceral Technoscience, and Liberatory Imagination in Everyday Life,* ed. Ruha Benjamin, 252–74. Durham, N.C.: Duke University Press.

Gaskins, Nettrice. 2021. *Techno-Vernacular Creativity and Innovation: Culturally Relevant Making inside and outside of the Classroom*. Cambridge, Mass.: MIT Press.

Goffman, Erving. 1959. *The Presentation of Self in Everyday Life*. New York: Anchor Books.

Gosse, Johanna, and Timothy Stott, eds. 2021. *Nervous Systems: Art, Systems, and Politics since the 1960s*. Durham, N.C.: Duke University Press.

Gregory, Sam. 2015. "Ubiquitous Witnesses: Who Creates the Evidence and the Live(d) Experience of Human Rights Violations?" *Information, Communication & Society* 18, no. 11 (August): 1378–92. https://doi.org/10.1080/1369118X.2015.1070891.

Grosz, Elizabeth. 2012. "Identity and Individuation: Some Feminist Reflections." In *Gilbert Simondon: Being and Technology*, ed. Arne De Boever, Alex Murray, Jon Roffe, and Ashley Woodward, trans. Arne De Boever, 37–56. Edinburgh: Edinburgh University Press.

Guarriello, Nicholas-Brie. 2019. "Never Give up, Never Surrender: Game Live Streaming, Neoliberal Work, and Personalized Media Economies." *New Media & Society* 21, no. 8 (March): 1750–69. https://doi.org/10.1177/1461444819831653.

Hamad, Ruby. 2020. *White Tears/Brown Scars: How White Feminism Betrays Women of Color*. New York: Catapult.

Hartman, Saidiya. 1997. *Scenes of Subjection: Terror, Slavery, and Self-Making in Nineteenth-Century America*. Race and American Culture. New York: Oxford University Press.

Hartman, Saidiya. 2007. *Lose Your Mother: A Journey along the Atlantic Slave Route*. New York: Farrar, Straus, and Giroux.

Hayles, N. Katherine. 2007. "Hyper and Deep Attention: The Generational Divide in Cognitive Modes." *Profession 189 (December)*: 187–99.

Hsieh, Tehching, and Adrian Heathfield. 2015. *Out of Now: The Lifeworks of Tehching Hsieh*. Cambridge, Mass.: MIT Press.

Hui, Yuk. 2016. *On the Existence of Digital Objects*. Minneapolis: University of Minnesota Press.

Hui, Yuk. 2021. *Art and Cosmotechnics*. Minneapolis: E-flux.

Hunter, Lindsay Brandon. 2019. "Live Streaming and the Perils of Proximity." *International Journal of Performance Arts and Digital Media* 15, no. 3: 283–94. https://doi.org/10.1080/14794713.2019.1671697.

Hunter, Lindsay Brandon. 2021. *Playing Real: Mimesis, Media, and Mischief*. Evanston, Ill.: Northwestern University Press.

Jackson, Sarah J., Moya Bailey, and Brooke Foucault Welles. 2020. *#hashtagactivism: Networks of Race and Gender Justice*. Cambridge, Mass.: MIT Press.

Kane, Carolyn L. 2019. *High-Tech Trash: Glitch, Noise, and Aesthetic Failure*. Oakland, Calif.: University of California Press.

Kant, Immanuel. 2000. *Critique of the Power of Judgment*. Cambridge: Cambridge University Press.

Kavada, Anastasia, and Emiliano Treré. 2020. "Live Democracy and Its Tensions: Making Sense of Livestreaming in the 15M and Occupy." *Information, Communication & Society* 23, no. 12: 1787–1804. https://doi .org/10.1080/1369118X.2019.1637448.

Knight, Brooke A. 2000. "Watch Me! Webcams and the Public Exposure of Private Lives." *Art Journal* 59, no. 4: 21. https://doi.org/10.2307/778117.

Krotoski, Aleks, dir. 2016. "Jennifer." *The Digital Human*. https://www.bbc .co.uk/programmes/b07z414z.

Kumanyika, Chenjerai. 2017. "Livestreaming in the Black Lives Matter Network." In *DIY Utopia: Cultural Imagination and the Remaking of the Possible*, ed. Amber Day, 169–88. Blue Ridge Summit, Penn.: Lexington Books.

Leonard, Marion. 2017. *Gender in the Music Industry: Rock, Discourse, and Girl Power*. London: Routledge.

Loveless, Natalie S. 2013. "The Materiality of Duration: Between Ice Time and Water Time." *Performance Research* 18, no. 6: 129–36.

Lynch, Kathleen. 2022. *Care and Capitalism: Why Affective Equality Matters for Social Justice*. Medford: Polity Press.

Machhi, Jatin, Jonathan Herskovitz, Ahmed M. Senan, Debashis Dutta, Barnali Nath, Maxim D. Oleynikov, Wilson R. Blomberg, Douglas D. Meigs, Mahmudul Hasan, Milankumar Patel, Peter Kline, Raymond Chuen-Chung Chang, Linda Chang, Howard E. Gendelman, and Bhavesh D. Kevadiya. 2020. "The Natural History, Pathobiology, and Clinical Manifestations of SARS-CoV-2 Infections." *Journal of Neuroimmune Pharmacology*, 15 (July): 359–86. https://doi.org/10.1007 /s11481-020-09944-5.

Maguire, Emma. 2018. *Girls, Autobiography, Media: Gender and Self-Mediation in Digital Economies*. Cham, Switz.: Palgrave Macmillan.

Martini, Michele. 2018. "Online Distant Witnessing and Live-Streaming Activism: Emerging Differences in the Activation of Networked Publics." *New Media & Society* 20, no. 11: 4035–55. https://doi.org/10 .1177/1461444818766703.

Massumi, Brian. 2012. "'Technical Mentality' Revisted: Brian Massumi on Gilbert Simondon." In *Gilbert Simondon: Being and Technology*, ed. Arne De Boever, Alex Murray, Jon Roffe, and Ashley Woodward, trans. Arne De Boever, 19–36. Edinburgh: Edinburgh University Press.

Masura, Nadja. 2020. *Digital Theatre: The Making and Meaning of Live Mediated Performance, US & UK 1990–2020*. Palgrave Studies in Performance and Technology. Cham, Switz.: Palgrave Macmillan.

McIlwain, Charlton D. 2020. *Black Software: The Internet and Racial Justice, from the AfroNet to Black Lives Matter*. New York: Oxford University Press.

Mckenzie, Mia. 2015. "How to Tell the Difference Between Real Solidarity and 'Ally Theater.'" *Black Girl Dangerous* (blog). November 4, 2015. https://www.blackgirldangerous.com/2015/11/ally-theater/.

Michaud, Yves. 2012. "The Aesthetics of Gilbert Simondon: Anticipation of the Contemporary Aesthetic Experience." In *Gilbert Simondon: Being and Technology*, ed. Arne De Boever, Alex Murray, Jon Roffe, and Ashley Woodward, trans. Justin Clemens, 121–32. Edinburgh: Edinburgh University Press.

Miller, Daniel, and Jolynna Sinanan. 2014. *Webcam*. Cambridge: Polity.

Nevin, Matthew. 2020. "Matt's Chats—How One Irish Gallery Took the Conversation Online." RTE Culture. June 9, 2020. https://www.rte.ie/culture/2020/0602/1144925-matts-chats-how-one-irish-gallery-took-the-conversation-online/.

Noble, Safiya Umoja. 2018. "Critical Surveillance Literacy in Social Media: Interrogating Black Death and Dying Online." *Black Camera* 9, no. 2: 147. https://doi.org/10.2979/blackcamera.9.2.10.

O'Dwyer, Néill. 2021. *Digital Scenography: Thirty Years of Experimentation and Innovation in Performance and Interactive Media*. Performance + Design. London: Bloomsbury Methuen Drama.

Puig de la Bellacasa, María. 2017. *Matters of Care: Speculative Ethics in More than Human Worlds*. Minneapolis: University of Minnesota Press.

Putnam, EL. 2022. *The Maternal, Digital Subjectivity, and the Aesthetics of Interruption*. New York: Bloomsbury Academic.

Rancière, Jacques. 2014. *The Politics of Aesthetics: The Distribution of the Sensible*. London: Bloomsbury.

Rancière, Jacques. 2016. "Béla Tarr: The Poetics and the Politics of Fiction." In *Slow Cinema*, ed. Tiago De Luca and Nuno Barradas Jorge, 245–60. Traditions in World Cinema. Edinburgh: Edinburgh University Press.

Rancière, Jacques. 2019. *Aisthesis: Scenes from the Aesthetic Regime of Art*. Trans. Zakir Paul. London: Verso.

Rodney, Seph. 2020. "What It Takes to Raise a Black Woman Up." *The New York Times*, June 19, 2020. https://www.nytimes.com/2020/06/19/arts/design/ayana-evans-black-women.html.

Russell, Legacy. 2020. *Glitch Feminism: A Manifesto*. London: Verso.

Salter, Chris. 2010. *Entangled: Technology and the Transformation of Performance*. Cambridge, Mass.: MIT Press.

Senft, Theresa M. 2008. *Camgirls: Celebrity and Community in the Age of Social Networks*. Digital Formations 4. New York: Lang.

shakur, fayemi. 2018. "A Performance Artist's Tests of Endurance Honor the Black Female Body." Hyperallergic. June 21, 2018. http://hyperallergic.com/448242/ayana-evans-medium-tings-performance/.

Shannon, Claude. 1948. "A Mathematical Theory of Communication." *The Bell System Technical Journal* 27, no. 3: 379–423.

Sharpe, Christina Elizabeth. 2016. *In the Wake: On Blackness and Being.* Durham, N.C.: Duke University Press.

Simondon, Gilbert. 2012. "On Techno-Aesthetics." Trans. Arne De Boever. *Parrhesia* 14: 1–8.

Simondon, Gilbert. 2014. *Imagination et invention: 1965–1966.* Ed. Nathalie Simondon and Jean-Yves Chateau. Paris: PUF.

Simondon, Gilbert. 2016. *On the Mode of Existence of Technical Objects.* Minneapolis: Univocal Pub.

Simondon, Gilbert. 2020. *Individuation in Light of Notions of Form and Information.* Trans. Taylor Adkins. Minneapolis: University of Minnesota Press.

Simondon, Gilbert. 2022. *Imagination and Invention.* Trans. Joe Hughes and Christophe Wall-Romana. Minneapolis: University of Minnesota Press.

Sontag, Susan. 2003. *Regarding the Pain of Others.* New York: Picador.

Stiegler, Bernard. 2014. *Symbolic Misery: The Hyperindustrial Epoch.* Trans. Barnaby Norman. Malden, Mass.: Polity Press.

Suchman, Lucille Alice. 2007. *Human-Machine Reconfigurations: Plans and Situated Actions.* Cambridge: Cambridge University Press.

Sutherland, Tonia. 2017. "Making a Killing: On Race, Ritual, and (Re) Membering in Digital Culture." *Preservation, Digital Technology & Culture* 46, no. 1: 32–40. https://doi.org/10.1515/pdtc-2017-0025.

Taylor, T. L. 2018. *Watch Me Play: Twitch and the Rise of Game Live Streaming.* Princeton Studies in Culture and Technology. Princeton: Princeton University Press.

Thorburn, Elise Danielle. 2014. "Social Media, Subjectivity, and Surveillance: Moving on From Occupy, the Rise of Live Streaming Video." *Communication and Critical/Cultural Studies* 11, no. 1: 52–63. https://doi.org/10.1080/14791420.2013.827356.

Tran, Christine H. 2021. "Stream(Age) Queens: Zoom-Bombs, Glitter Bombs & Other Doctoral Fairy Tales." *Communication, Culture, and Critique* 14, no. 2: 356–60. https://doi.org/10.1093/ccc/tcab028.

Wark, McKenzie. 2019. *Capital Is Dead.* London: Verso.

Weaver, Warren. 1949. "Recent Contributions to the Mathematical Theory of Communication." In *The Mathematical Theory of Communication,* by Claude Shannon and Warren Weaver, 1–28. Chicago: University of Chicago Press.

White, Michele. 2003. "Too Close to See: Men, Women, and Webcams." *New Media & Society* 5, no. 1: 7–28. https://doi.org/10.1177/1461444803005001901.

White, Michele. 2006. *The Body and the Screen: Theories of Internet Spectatorship.* Cambridge, Mass.: MIT Press.

Woodcock, Jamie, and Mark R. Johnson. 2019. "The Affective Labor and Performance of Live Streaming on Twitch.Tv." *Television & New Media* 20, no. 8: 813–23. https://doi.org/10.1177/1527476419851077.

Wu, Tim. 2016. *The Attention Merchants: The Epic Scramble to Get Inside Our Heads.* New York: Vintage Books.

Zhang, Ge, and Larissa Hjorth. 2019. "Live-Streaming, Games, and Politics of Gender Performance: The Case of *Nüzhubo* in China." *Convergence: The International Journal of Research into New Media Technologies* 25, no. 5–6: 807–25. https://doi.org/10.1177/1354856517738160.

Zuboff, Shoshana. 2019. *The Age of Surveillance Capitalism: The Fight for a Human Future at the New Frontier of Power.* New York: PublicAffairs.

(Continued from page iii)

Forerunners: Ideas First

Claudia Milian
LatinX

Aaron Jaffe
Spoiler Alert: A Critical Guide

Don Ihde
Medical Technics

Jonathan Beecher Field
Town Hall Meetings and the Death of Deliberation

Jennifer Gabrys
How to Do Things with Sensors

Naa Oyo A. Kwate
**Burgers in Blackface: Anti-Black Restaurants
Then and Now**

Arne De Boever
Against Aesthetic Exceptionalism

Steve Mentz
Break Up the Anthropocene

John Protevi
Edges of the State

Matthew J. Wolf-Meyer
**Theory for the World to Come: Speculative Fiction and
Apocalyptic Anthropology**

Nicholas Tampio
Learning versus the Common Core

Kathryn Yusoff
A Billion Black Anthropocenes or None

Kenneth J. Saltman
The Swindle of Innovative Educational Finance

Ginger Nolan
The Neocolonialism of the Global Village

Joanna Zylinska
The End of Man: A Feminist Counterapocalypse

Robert Rosenberger
Callous Objects: Designs against the Homeless

William E. Connolly
**Aspirational Fascism: The Struggle for Multifaceted
Democracy under Trumpism**

Chuck Rybak
UW Struggle: When a State Attacks Its University

Clare Birchall
Shareveillance: The Dangers of Openly Sharing and Covertly Collecting Data

la paperson
A Third University Is Possible

Kelly Oliver
Carceral Humanitarianism: Logics of Refugee Detention

P. David Marshall
The Celebrity Persona Pandemic

Davide Panagia
Ten Theses for an Aesthetics of Politics

David Golumbia
The Politics of Bitcoin: Software as Right-Wing Extremism

Sohail Daulatzai
Fifty Years of *The Battle of Algiers*: Past as Prologue

Gary Hall
The Uberfication of the University

Mark Jarzombek
Digital Stockholm Syndrome in the Post-Ontological Age

N. Adriana Knouf
How Noise Matters to Finance

Andrew Culp
Dark Deleuze

Akira Mizuta Lippit
Cinema without Reflection: Jacques Derrida's Echopoiesis and Narcissism Adrift

Sharon Sliwinski
Mandela's Dark Years: A Political Theory of Dreaming

Grant Farred
Martin Heidegger Saved My Life

Ian Bogost
The Geek's Chihuahua: Living with Apple

Shannon Mattern
Deep Mapping the Media City

Steven Shaviro
No Speed Limit: Three Essays on Accelerationism

Jussi Parikka
The Anthrobscene

Reinhold Martin
Mediators: Aesthetics, Politics, and the City

John Hartigan Jr.
Aesop's Anthropology: A Multispecies Approach

EL Putnam is assistant professor in digital media at Maynooth University in Ireland and the author of *The Maternal, Digital Subjectivity, and the Aesthetics of Interruption* (Bloomsbury 2022).